PAYING FOR BETTER TEACHING:
Merit Pay and Its Alternatives

by Samuel B. Bacharach, David B. Lipsky,
and Joseph B. Shedd.
With the assistance of K. Haydn Wood.

Organizational Analysis and Practice, Inc.
Boardman House, 120 East Buffalo St., Ithaca, N.Y. 14850

Bacharach, Samuel B.
    Paying for better teaching.

    Bibliography: p.
    1. Teachers—Salaries, pensions, etc.—United States.
    2. Compensation management—United States.
I. Lipsky, David B., 1939-   . II. Shedd, Joseph B.   III. Title.
LB2842.2.B32 1984   331.2'81371100973   84-1096

    ISBN 0-930475-00-3

Cover design by Jim Powers

Published in the United States of America.
Second Printing

The Authors

Samuel B. Bacharach is Professor and Chairman of the Department of Organizational Behavior in Cornell University's New York State School of Industrial and Labor Relations. His research includes work on compensation, job analysis, organizational design, quality of work life, bargaining, and educational administration. He has published widely in scholarly journals, and he is the author or editor of six books, including *Organizational Behavior in Schools and School Districts* and the annual JAI Press Series, *Research in The Sociology of Organizations*. He has served on the Editorial Board and as Book Review Editor for *Administrative Science Quarterly*.

David B. Lipsky is Professor and Chairman of the Department of Collective Bargaining, Labor Law, and Labor History in Cornell University's New York State School of Industrial and Labor Relations. His research includes work on teacher compensation and labor relations in public education, and he has served as mediator, fact-finder, or arbitrator in numerous public education bargaining disputes. He has published widely in scholarly journals, and is the author of several books, including *Unfinished Business: An Agenda for Labor, Management, and the Public, Union Power and Public Policy*, and *Advances in Industrial and Labor Relations*. He has served as Co-Director of the Institute of Employment and Training Administration at Harvard University and as Editor and Associate Editor of the *Industrial and Labor Relations Review*.

Joseph B. Shedd is Lecturer and a doctoral candidate in the Department of Collective Bargaining, Labor Law, and Labor History within the New York State School of Industrial and Labor Relations at Cornell. His research and publications include work on teacher compensation, collective bargaining in public education, public sector labor law, and bargaining theory. Before returning to Cornell for his doctorate, he served for six years as a management representative and labor relations specialist for the Federal Government.

K. Haydn Wood completed his master's degree in the Department of Organizational Behavior at the New York State School of Industrial and Labor Relations, Cornell University, and he is now a Research Associate for Organizational Analysis and Practice, Inc. His recent work has focused on needs assessments and program evaluations, through conducting and analyzing large-scale surveys. His previous research centered around the promotion of employee participation and motivation through the design of compensation and decision-making systems.

Samuel Bacharach and David Lipsky are also Senior Consultants, and Joseph Shedd a Research Associate, for Organizational Analysis and Practice, Inc. OAP is a research and consulting group specializing in the practical application of organizational science, based in Ithaca, New York. It focuses on areas such as compensation administration, human resource use, personnel strategy, work processes, and quality of work life. OAP's services range from diagnosis through design and implementation. OAP is also a publisher of practitioner-oriented monographs on critical issues in the fields in which it consults.

The authors gratefully acknowledge the assistance of Scott Bauer for his help in the early stages of their research on merit pay, and thank Faith White for her meticulous typing and ever-present good humour.

Contents

Page

The Definition of Merit Pay 2

What Merit Pay Is Not 3

Arguments In Favor of Merit Pay 4

    Incentive 5

    Reward 6

    Feedback... 6

    Control, Coordination and

        Administrator Involvement........................... 7

    Retention in the Profession 9

    Retention in the Classroom 10

    Recruitment... 10

    Raising Public Spending on Education................. 12

Arguments Against Merit Pay 13

    Incentives and Approaches to Teaching................ 16

    Incentives and Motivation 17

    Impact on Working Relationships

        Among Teachers..................................... 20

    Impact on Teacher-Administrator Relations 22

    Impact on School-Parent Relations..................... 24

    Judgmental Versus Diagnostic Feedback............... 24

    Impact on Staff Development 25

    Measuring Performance 26

    Teacher Recruitment 30

    Teacher Turnover 31

Administrative Burden 33

Overall Costs 34

Collective Bargaining Issues............................ 35

Weighing the Theoretical Arguments

Against Actual Experience with Merit Plans.................. 37

Alternatives: Retaining the Unified

Salary Schedule 39

Alternatives: Reforms Within the Unified

Salary Schedule 42

Consolidating Increments 42

Increase the Overall Rewards for Experience.......... 42

Restrictions on Credited Courses 43

Salary Credits for In-Service Education 43

Pay for Retraining in Shortage Subject Areas 43

Alternatives: Making Exceptions to the

Unified Salary Schedule 44

Special Recruitment Rates for Teachers

in Shortage Categories 44

Pre-Dismissal Witholding of Step Increases............ 46

Group Bonus Plans...................................... 48

Alternatives: Career Ladders and

Career Promotions 50

The Tenure Decision as a Career Step................. 52

Pre-Tenure Internships 53

Sabbatic Leave 54

Senior Teacher System................................. 55

Alternatives: Goal-Oriented Management and

    Participation Systems 58

Appendices

A. Major Reports on Education, 1983 64

B. Relationships Between Average Beginning
Salary Offers of Bachelor's Degree Candidates
Entering Business and Industry, By Curriculum,
and Average Minimum Salaries of Teachers with
a Bachelor's Degree, 1973-74 to 1980-81 66

C. Relationships Between Average Beginning
Salary Offers of Inexperienced Master's
Degree Candidates Entering Business and
Industry, By Curriculum, and Average Minimum
Salaries For Teachers with a Master's Degree,
1973-74 to 1980-81 67

D. Comparison of Teacher Minimum and Maximum
Annual Salaries with Annual Salaries of Other
Professional, Administrative, Technical, and
Clerical Positions, March 1979 68

Bibliography 70

PAYING FOR BETTER TEACHING: Merit Pay and Its Alternatives

America wants to upgrade its education system. Parents, legislators, investigatory commissions, teaching professionals and many others have called for higher standards in U.S. education, particularly in primary and secondary schools. The problems have been thoroughly described by multiple commissions and expert studies. (See summary in Appendix A.) Everyone agrees that we must have change. But what changes are needed, and how are they to be achieved?

In the most publicized report advocating education reform, entitled *A Nation At Risk*, the National Commission on Excellence in Education identified many problems and proposed many possible solutions. President Reagan embraced one of these possibilities — merit pay — and advocated its adoption as the main vehicle for education change. He argued that "We spend more money per child for education than any other country in the world — we just aren't getting our money's worth... Teachers should be paid and promoted on the basis of their merit... Hard-earned tax dollars should encourage the best. They have no business rewarding incompetence and mediocrity" (*Washington Post*, May 22, 1983).

The President's argument and attempts to implement merit pay have prompted a sharp debate. Advocates and opponents have flung arguments (and accusations) back and forth. Too frequently, however, the sides have talked past one another: each group points to the benefits of its position, and the costs of its opponent's position, without seriously trying to weigh both. This book is intended to raise the level of the debate. We attempt to lay out objectively the arguments for and against merit pay, and to assess its relative worth as a means of raising the quality of U.S. education.

1

We begin with a clarification of the merit pay concept. The arguments in favor of merit pay are then detailed. These include discussion of merit pay as a means of:

- Incentive
- Feedback
- Reward
- Control, Coordination, and Administrator Involvement

- Retention in the Profession
- Retention in the Classroom
- Recruitment
- Raising Public Spending on Education

The arguments against merit pay follow, covering:

- Incentives and Teaching Approaches
- Incentives and Motivation
- Impact on Working Relationships Among Teachers
- Impact on Teacher-Administrator Relations
- Impact on Parent-School Relations

- Judgmental Versus Diagnostic Feedback
- Impact on Staff Development
- Issues in Measuring Teacher Performance
- Teacher Recruitment
- Teacher Turnover
- Administrative Burden
- Overall Costs
- Collective Bargaining Issues

The next section weighs both sides against historical experience, and the last several sections discuss alternative approaches to improving the compensation and management systems in public education.

The Definition of Merit Pay

Part of the confusion in the debate results from muddied definitions of the merit pay concept. Merit pay is a general concept with many variations, and as a political label it has been applied to many different and unrelated compensation proposals. This discussion focuses specifically on **standard merit pay: a compensation system that links the salaries of individual teachers to evaluations of their performance.** "**Old Style**" standard merit pay generally ties salaries to assessments of the form and content of a teacher's activities in the classroom. "**New Style**" standard merit pay normally ties salaries to student scores on standardized tests.

There are many variations on the merit pay theme. It can, for example, either replace or be implemented via the structure of the unified salary schedule. "Meritorious" teachers may receive double or triple increments, thus accelerating their movement up a salary schedule. Alternatively, the merit payment could come in the form of bonuses allocated by the local board of education, or the plan may allow selected teachers to earn more than the maximum level in a schedule. Evaluation of a teacher's performance can be undertaken by a principal acting alone, by a lower level administrator, by the teacher's peers, or by some combination of these three. A handful of merit pay plans also give weight to student evaluations. Multiple variations also exist in other aspects of merit pay schemes, such as in the size and timing of payments. Still, the central elements of the merit pay concept are clear, and the discussion need only focus on these. (See Educational Research Service, 1979, pp. 1-4 for further description of the various forms of merit pay.)

What Merit Pay is Not

Unlike merit pay, **master teacher** plans are not compensation systems. Rather, they are job structures with compensation implications. The master teacher approach aims at increasing the levels and complexity of the hierarchy in a school, in order to construct better career paths for teachers. Outstanding teachers are appointed to positions that combine classroom activity with responsibility for aiding and leading other teachers. Less trained and less experienced staff are assigned to lower level positions, with the opportunity to move into more professional activities when they have shown their worth. Proponents usually argue that compensation levels should parallel the steps of the career path.

The arguments for this approach differ importantly from those supporting merit pay. They are based on the idea that provision of a career path, rather than specifically pay increases contingent on performance, will motivate teachers. Still, because variations in pay normally accompany such schemes, and because the variations are supposed to reflect the person's value in achieving school goals, the outcome resembles merit pay in some respects. Many of the points made below will apply to master teacher plans as well as to merit pay.

Differentiated staffing plans are a close cousin to master teacher plans. The only real difference is the greater generality of differentiated staffing plans: they are explicitly intended to cover the entire teacher staff, with less emphasis particularly on the master teacher position. In all major respects, however, the two plans are synonomous.

Another proposed reform, the **speciality-linked salary schedule**, is intended to deal with teacher shortages in particular subject areas — at present, mathematics, science, and special education. Such schedules are generally implemented by paying higher entry-level salaries to teachers in specialities that command higher salaries in non-education labor markets. It is a compensation approach, but it ignores consideration of teacher motivation, teacher performance, and the internal (within school) equity of pay relationships. It focuses exclusively on external labor market considerations.

Work environment premiums, sometimes called "combat pay," are often paid to teachers in especially difficult working conditions such as inner-city schools and schools for the handicapped. Again, these differ from merit pay, because they are not pay-for-perfomance/incentive systems.

Group bonus plans, such as that contained in the "Second Mile" program in Houston, Texas, overlap importantly with the merit pay concept. Consequently, many of the arguments below will apply to that approach. The obvious difference is that the standard merit pay idea is based on evaluating and commensurately rewarding **individual** teachers. The so-called "merit pay" component of the Houston plan measures performance and allocates benefits on a **group** (school-wide) basis. Group bonus plans can vary in their unit of measurement, ranging from groups of teachers up to district-wide or even state-wide plans, but all differ from standard merit plans in the same way: they do not concentrate on individual teacher performance.

Special recognition and **special bonus** plans also exist in many school districts — outstanding teacher awards and so on. These differ from true merit pay schemes to the extent that they do not continually link all teachers' salaries to evaluations of performance.

Arguments in Favor of Merit Pay

Most of the arguments for merit pay can be summarized in two words: **money motivates**. Advocates believe that linking financial rewards to assessments of performance will increase motivation where it is lacking, sustain motivation where it might otherwise slip, strengthen evaluation and feedback mechanisms, and give principals and other administrators the tools they need to exercise strong leadership. In the process, principals will have a concrete means of communicating goals they expect their teachers to achieve, teachers' commitment to standards of excellence will increase, and their performance will improve.

The argument that merit pay will serve all these ends depends on three fundamental assumptions: (a) achieving better teacher performance is essentially a motivational issue; (b) making salary contingent on performance will provide the needed motivation; (c) teacher performance can be adequately measured. If all three assumptions are accepted, then the rationale for adopting a merit pay system is a powerful one; districts might still have problems devising a system that puts these assumptions into practice, but these would be technical problems which might be overcome given sufficient expertise, time, determination, and money.

Incentive

At the simplest but probably most persuasive level, merit pay supporters argue that **teachers will raise their performance if offered a pay raise for doing so.** Teachers have aims they want to fulfill, money can help them in meeting these aims. Providing a path to obtaining more money will result in teachers following that path. If the path is defined as higher performance, teachers will act accordingly. They will put in extra time and effort, improve their training, and demand higher standards both of themselves and their students. William Casey (1979), for example, argues at length that teachers are no different from workers in other occupations in which money is effective as an incentive. If financial reward is the basic reason for working as a teacher, better teacher performances should be brought about by making teachers' salary increases contingent on their performance levels.

At a more sophisticated level, merit pay proponents acknowledge that money is not the only motivator, especially in an occupation like teaching. They realize that "intrinsic" motivators, such as interest in the process of teaching for its own sake, are also important. Still, while taking these into account, the advocates believe that **extra money will necessarily add to the reasons to be a better teacher**. It will be another reason to go the extra mile.

Reward

Some advocates of merit pay support the system because it is a means of **rewarding teachers who already perform excellently**. Many teachers already contribute superlative effort and achievement, but they are discouraged, it is claimed, when they see that other less committed teachers receive the same compensation for their efforts. A merit pay plan is intended to identify and reward outstanding individuals. Conversely, those who are not contributing at a high level will not receive any additional benefit. Thus merit pay will produce a more equitable distribution of the financial benefits of teaching. Those who perform excellently will be rewarded, those who do not, will not.

In contrast to the incentive argument, this position does not assert that merit pay will **increase** the individual teacher's standard of performance. Rather, advocates using this argument believe that it will maintain overall standards of performance by preventing some teachers' standards from declining. Teachers who already perform excellently will be encouraged to maintain their efforts. Although the claims of merit pay advocates often focus on using the plan to raise individual performance, school districts actually using merit pay more often cite its benefit as a reward system rather than as an incentive system (Educational Research Service, 1979).

Feedback

Clearly the system of incentives and/or rewards in a merit plan will give **feedback to teachers about their individual performance**. Those who receive merit payments will know to continue their good work. Others will be shown the need to change. Lortie (1975) and Jackson (1968) present compelling evidence that teachers frequently are unsure when their efforts have been effective. A number of studies have documented that teachers value recognition from their administrators and peers in large part because it provides feedback on what they are doing. Teachers who report that they have received such feedback are more satisfied with their work and their careers than those who have not (Chapman and Lowther, 1982).

Merit pay provides administrators with additional opportunities to give feedback to teachers, and gives them greater incentive to strengthen the evaluation procedures that generate such feedback. Merit plans also give teachers an additional reason to pay attention to the feedback. Research indicates that many teachers find that their training in education methods was insufficient to prepare them for the demands of the classroom. There is a widespread belief that a person can best "become a teacher by being a teacher". This conviction may be a source of reassurance to new teachers and a source of pride for more experienced ones, but it is hardly grounds for rejoicing. It implies that beginners must undergo an inefficient, trial-and-error process of searching for the best technique, without being able to draw on the insights of others who have already experienced such a process. It also implies that more experienced teachers may content themselves with what seem to be satisfactory solutions to recurring problems, rather than continuing to search for even better solutions, simply because they have no way of knowing how much more (or less) success they might have if they were to try something else.

The motivation problem caused by insufficient feedback is not that teachers will not want to perform well. Instead it is that **there is too much opportunity — and too much incentive — for teachers to define their own standards of effectiveness**. These standards can allow them to conclude that they have performed well, when more demanding criteria and more critical assessments of performance might reveal ways in which they could improve.

Control, Coordination, and Administrator Involvement

The process of education is not what **one** teacher provides to his or her students. Rather, it is what a **group** of teachers provides to children over at least twelve or thirteen years. The attitudes and learning skills which students acquire in one classroom have a direct effect on what other teachers are subsequenty able to accomplish. The knowledge they acquire from one teacher will prepare them — or not prepare them — for the material that other teachers are expected to impart. Unless the efforts of these teachers are integrated, the effectiveness of their collective and individual efforts will be seriously undermined.

Probably the single most important observation generated by researchers who have studied "effective schools" is that their administrators and teachers are significantly more likely to treat education as a collegial effort, directed toward common goals, rather than as a process conducted in individual classrooms (see Little, 1982; Leithwood and Montgomery, 1982). There is a **coherence** to the efforts of those who work in effective schools that is not found in other schools (Wynne, 1981). The fact that schools differ in the extent to which the efforts of their various members are integrated and focused is an indication that such coherence cannot be taken for granted. The observation that teachers and administrators in effective schools do not take this coherence for granted, but work hard to develop goals and programs with a school-wide focus, is probably the closest "effective schools" researchers have come to providing guidelines for improving the quality of education in our schools.

Merit pay, its proponents contend, **will give administrators a powerful tool to achieve coordination**. The tool will primarily operate through the feedback mechanism discussed in the previous section, but differs from straightforward feedback in its emphasis on deliberate administrator influence in the system. Feedback can only reward behaviors if they have occurred, whereas administrators can use a merit pay plan to **introduce new methods and aims**. A principal can introduce a change and reward those who put extra effort toward achieving it.

Lortie (1975) has noted that the pursuit of intrinsic satisfactions in the classroom sometimes leads teachers to concentrate on doing those things they are most likely to be personally successful in accomplishing, which may or may not serve the interests of the school district as a whole. Principals and school boards can have little influence over intrinsic motivation, but increasing the importance of an extrinsic motivator (money), which can be varied at the administrator's discretion, may give them **more control over the process of teaching**.

Additionally, one of the more important, if subtle, attractions of merit pay is that it forces administrators to pay attention to what their teachers are doing in the classroom. It requires them to enter the classrooms, because they need adequate observations to judge performance. None of the literature on merit pay, of which we are aware, makes this point. Still, our experience and research in schools indicates that **increasing administrator involvement in day-to-day teaching** could be a major advantage of merit pay plans.

Retention in the Profession

The reward and feedback mechanisms of a merit pay system should reduce turnover among a district's most valuable teachers, supporters of the concept argue. Excellent teachers, it is said, realize and resent the fact that they are not rewarded for their efforts in the form of higher salaries. Consequently, they are leaving teaching and going into occupations in which their contributions will be "appreciated" (Kershaw & McKean, 1962).

Job-dissatisfaction and turnover are highly correlated, as substantial evidence documents (see Porter and Steers, 1973; Vroom, 1964; Hulin, 1968). But what **is** "job satisfaction" or "dissatisfaction" other than someone's score on a researcher's questionnaire? The answer most often used in discussions of turnover is provided by equity theory (Homans, 1961; Adams, 1965). Persons are assumed to compare the contributions they make and the rewards they receive with the contribution/reward ratios of other organization members. If the two ratios are not identical (or nearly so), then the organization member will conclude that he or she, or the comparison person, is being treated inequitably. If this is the case, the organization member will feel dissatisfied and will be prompted to reduce the feeling of inequity — perhaps by resigning. Similarly, persons may compare the contribution/reward ratio in their occupation with the ratios in other occupations, and switch occupations if their own ratio is perceived as inequitable and if the crossover is possible.

Merit pay advocates believe that **teachers who put in extra effort but are compensated on a unified salary schedule will see their rewards as inequitable** vis-a-vis those of the other teachers. (Under the unified schedule, all teachers with the same education and experience normally receive the same salary.) Unfortunately no research in teaching directly addresses this issue, although studies have shown that teachers who leave the profession are concerned about pay issues, and compare their pay with that of other professions. Male teachers are especially likely to make such comparisons (Mason, 1961; Lortie, 1975; Chapman and Lowther, 1982).

Strictly speaking, cross-occupation equity comparisons are more a matter of salary **levels** than of salary **structuring methods** such as merit pay. A merit pay plan will not aid retention of teachers **as a whole**, except through possible secondary consequences such as raising the average teacher salary. Still, increasing the retention of all teachers is not the aim of merit pay proponents. They wish only to increase the retention rate of excellent (and perhaps average) teachers.

In addition to expecting merit pay to lower the resignation rate among the best teachers, a number of educators expect to employ it as a means of **increasing resignations among the low-performing teachers**. Many districts give merit increments to the majority of their teachers and only withold it from teachers who have performed below average. That is, the merit pay plan is employed as a means of **punishment** with the aim of urging the offending teachers to raise standards or leave. Districts can find it very difficult to dislodge a low-performing teacher through conventional channels, but a long-term relative decrease in their salaries may prompt resignation.

Retention in the Classroom

Rather than leaving the profession entirely, excellent teachers who perceive pay inequities may move into administration. Merit pay advocates assert that at present excellent teachers can only obtain better rewards, more in keeping with their contributions, by leaving the classroom. From the viewpoint of raising the quality of education, a paradox develops: the best teachers have to give up teaching. Supporters of merit pay believe that the system will resolve the paradox: **excellent teachers will be able to obtain better rewards and continue in the classroom.**

Recruitment

Recent and current participants in teacher education programs are reported to have alarmingly low Scholastic Aptitude Test scores (Weaver, 1979). Furthermore, scores on competency exams like the NTE have concerned educators (Vance and Schlechty, 1982). On the basis of such reports, it has been argued that "Teachers entering service today are not your basic first-stringers..." (*Phi Delta Kappan*, 1979). Rather, the field is said to be losing excellent candidates to other occupations. The unified salary schedule is offered as a partial explanation for these trends, which in turn have been said to contribute to the declining quality of our schools.

Merit pay may be able to raise the quality of recruits to the teaching profession by offering the possibility of higher pay for first class teachers. Those who are willing to invest in top-grade training, and intend to put in top-grade efforts, will have the possibility of higher earnings. The prospect of higher pay for top performers may make teaching more attractive vis-a-vis other professions, because the projected career earnings of those who believe they will receive merit pay will be higher. With the bias given by optimism and good intentions, many potential recruits may be steered toward teaching by the higher earnings offered by merit pay.

Notice, however, that as with retention in the profession the critical issue for recruitment is the relative level of compensation, not the structure of compensation *per se*. There is ample evidence that the salary levels in teaching are much lower than those available in occupations requiring comparable levels of education and training. Appendix B presents estimates of how teachers' salaries (BA minimum) compared with the starting salaries of those entering other occupations with a bachelor's degree from 1973-74 to 1980-81. Appendix C presents similar estimates for those entering teaching and other occupations with a master's degree. Appendix D presents additional comparisons of starting salaries, and also indicates how the salaries of teachers with maximum experience and education credits fare against the salaries of those who have progressed to higher levels in other occupations. All three tables illustrate the relatively low and/or declining salary status of teaching. Appendix D, for example, indicates that those who enter teaching with a bachelor's degree can expect starting salaries roughly the same as those in mid-level clerical and entry-level technical assistance positions, where college degrees are not required. By the **end** of their careers in teaching, they can expect their salaries to pull within the range of salaries received **at the beginning** of careers in other occupations which require specialized college training and which provide higher professional status.

Merit pay alone will not radically change these interoccupation differences in earnings, but it may substantially raise the earnings expectations held by ambitious potential teachers — those who believe they will qualify for merit increments. To the extent this is true, merit pay will help teacher recruitment. There is a danger in this line of argument, however, which some advocates of merit pay are quick to acknowledge and which others are inclined to ignore (Educational Research Service, 1979). **Merit pay cannot be treated as an alternative to raising average teacher salaries**. If higher levels of salary for some teachers come at the expense of lower salaries for others —if merit pay is treated as a means of "getting more without paying more" — there is little reason to expect that it will have any significant beneficial impact on teacher recruitment. In fact, since the levels of salary that new teachers would be **guaranteed** in salary offers may decline under such an approach, the impact on recruitment could well be negative. But if merit pay is funded by **new** monies that would not otherwise be available, thereby raising the absolute levels of pay in teaching, its impact on recruitment may well be positive.

Raising Public Spending on Education

Some educators support merit pay because it may be a feasible way of increasing public spending for education: **a vehicle for increasing education spending that is acceptable to the voting public**. These supporters often acknowledge possible problems with the merit pay approach. In particular, many believe that its overall cost will probably be higher than the current system, because of its administrative complexity and because "meritorious" teachers will be paid more while the "non-meritorious" will not be paid less (in absolute terms). If this is the case, the average teacher salary will rise. These advocates argue, however, that the increase will be accepted if the American public believes that a better system of education is being put in place. For example, new education legislation in Tennessee (with a merit pay component) includes a 1% rise in the State sales tax, but voters appear to have accepted the measure as necessary for education reform. The implication is that **voters will be more likely to accept increased spending if it is based on a new and politically popular approach**.

Merit pay supporters employing this argument see themselves as political realists. They want the education system to benefit from the current wave of public concern, and they fear that the possible benefits may be blocked by the public's disenchantment (justified or not) with current education compensation practices. Constituents of school districts will not vote for "more of the same", merit pay proponents argue, but they may vote for more funding if it accompanies a new idea. More money may be available if teachers are seen as working harder for it — if there is some assurance that better results will derive from the increase.

Arguments Against Merit Pay

Money can motivate. In certain work situations, making pay contingent on performance can improve performance. One major school of thought, using reinforcement theory (Skinner, 1969; Ayllon and Azrin, 1968), has produced several hundred studies showing that extrinsic rewards, such as money, will improve the performance of certain types of tasks (for reviews, see Kazdin, 1975; O'Leary and Drabman, 1971). On the other hand, an opposing "negative effects" school, drawing on several theories, has generated evidence that extrinsic rewards can **harm** motivation and performance in many situations (see Deci, 1976; Lepper and Greene, 1978).

Consequently, a core question in this section is: which of these findings applies to teaching? Is teaching a context in which a pay-for-performance system will harm or help motivation and performance? To answer these and related questions, it will be helpful to begin by summarizing key research literature on compensation, motivation, and performance. We then develop specific arguments concerning teacher motivation and performance, followed by discussion of practical implementation issues — especially the problems of measuring teacher performance.

To begin with, the apparent conflict between the two sets of findings referred to above is deceptive. Laboratory and field tests of reinforcement theory have almost always entailed tasks that in themselves were uninteresting or otherwise unattractive. Further, the tasks have all had "algorithmic" solutions: the people whose performance was being studied knew **what** they should accomplish and **how** to reach the goal. The second school, on the other hand, asked subjects to perform inherently interesting tasks with "heuristic" solutions: the goals and the means to accomplish them were not immediately obvious (McGraw, 1978). In other words, the conflict between the two sets of findings at leastly partly derives from the fact that they were measuring different kinds of performance.

Refinements of the research found that extrinsic rewards can aid the performance of algorithmic tasks that still maintain an inherent interest. Furthermore, the performance of initially heuristic tasks is not harmed, and is in some cases helped, by the offer of extrinsic rewards once the subjects have learned exactly how to perform the tasks. Thus, **the presence or absence of problem-solving appears to be the key factor in whether extrinsic rewards raise or lower performance.**

Several explanations are possible for these findings. Deci (1976) links intrinsic motivation to need satisfaction and "attributions of causality". Tasks which are interesting and challenging (i.e., they have heuristic solutions) provide opportunities for gaining self-confidence and a sense of accomplishment. Such intrinsic rewards will diminish, however, if the individual comes to attribute the reason for performing to an external source. If a person concludes that his or her behavior is being controlled by someone who is manipulating extrinsic rewards, her or his personal stake in performing well "for oneself" will be undermined. Deci and colleagues have conducted a number of studies that suggest that when the "controlling" aspect of extrinsic rewards is made salient, intrinsic motivation and subsequent performance at such tasks are negatively affected (see Deci, 1975).

Another group of scholars has built on the work of Festinger (1957), who noted that when individuals are asked to perform boring or otherwise unattractive tasks, they will hold negative attitudes towards those tasks so long as there is some "rational" explanation for performing them, such as receipt of extrinsic rewards. If such other explanations are not available, individuals tend to adjust their attitudes toward such tasks, finding them more attractive than they had previously. Festinger attributed such a change to "cognitive dissonance": people want to believe that there is some rational explanation for their behavior, and they will create an explanation if one is unavailable otherwise.

More recently, scholars have raised the possibility that such cognitive readjustments might be a more general phenomenon. Rather than assigning individuals tasks for which there is "insufficient justification", they have assigned them tasks for which there is "overly-sufficient justification" (i.e., tasks they initially perceive to be interesting and for which they are offered extrinsic rewards as well). These scholars have found that individuals' interest in the activity declines when there is some "outside" explanation for engaging in it, but their interest increases when such justification is removed. Festinger's explanation would have predicted the second adjustment but not the first (i.e., it would be perfectly "rational" to perform an activity because it was interesting **and** extrinsically rewarding).

Such findings suggest that individuals not only seek to explain their behavior: they also seek **parsimony** in their explanations. Conceivably, they might achieve parsimony by dismissing the importance of extrinsic rewards as a "cause" of their behavior. They are more likely, however, to adjust their perceptions of their interest in the activity — because they have more personal control over their perceived level of interest.

A third explanation of how extrinsic rewards might have negative effects on performance picks up where the second explanation leaves off. Condry and Chambers (1978) focus on how individuals actually go about performing tasks under extrinsic reward and non-reward conditions. Their basic argument is that when rewards are offered, individuals will concentrate on doing what is necessary to get them: "Attention is focused on the easiest route to [a] goal." When two paths could produce the same reward, but one is riskier and less certain of producing that reward, subjects choose the easier route. When an activity requires problem-solving, subjects offered extrinsic rewards are more likely to focus on finding the answer (and thus obtaining the reward) rather than understanding the problem. Subjects in a non-reward situation tend to learn more quickly, they make more efficient use of mistakes (asking themselves **why** an approach did not produce a solution), and they use fewer unsubstantiated guesses. "Intrinsically motivated subjects attend to and utilize a wider array of information; they are focused on the **way** to solve the problem rather than the solution. They are, in general, more careful, logical, and coherent in their problem-solving strategies than comparable subjects offered a reward to solve the same problems" (Condry and Chambers, 1978).

Condry and Chambers have also noted a difference in the willingness of reward and nonreward subjects to **re-engage** in an activity, once it has been initially completed. Those who have been rewarded for an activity are less likely to agree to engage in that activity in the future if the assurance of further rewards is withdrawn.

For these people, performance becomes **dependent** upon the reward system, whereas subjects who are not offered contingent rewards are normally willing to re-engage in an activity without being rewarded.

Incentives and Approaches to Teaching

One fairly clear conclusion from this body of research is that **pay-for-performance systems will increase the level of instrumental motivation among teachers**. Organization members adapt themselves to the established reward system, and teachers will tend to see students as a means to an end under merit pay. Student performance in classes or tests will be the main barrier between a teacher and a merit increment. This situation would be more pronounced under New Style merit pay, but even the evaluations used in Old Style systems are in large part dependent on pupil behavior.

To our knowledge, only one of the "negative effects" research studies looked at performance in a social setting, and its results are particularly relevant to merit pay and its effect on the classroom approaches adopted by teachers. Garbarino (1975) examined the effects of contingent rewards on the behavior of sixth-grade students who were asked to teach first-graders how to play a complicated but interesting game. Half of the sixth-graders (those in the "reward condition") were each offered a movie ticket if they could successfully teach the younger child how to play the game; the other sixth graders were asked to perform the same task, without the offer of a reward.

Garbarino found that the emotional tone of the interaction in the reward condition was significantly more negative: tutors criticized their tutees' mistakes and tutees themselves more often; they offered fewer positive evaluations of tutees themselves and only did so when the answers given were correct; they made more demands for answers; and they were less likely to engage in laughter. They were also more inclined to volunteer answers if answers were not immediately forthcoming.

The interaction in the non-reward context was positive on all these measures. When tutors in the non-reward condition criticized answers, they tended to couple these comments with positive information about the tutees themselves. As for the results of their efforts, non-reward tutors were significantly more successful: their tutees were more likely to achieve mastery of the game, in a shorter period of time, making fewer errors in the process.

While there are always limitations in generalizing from research efforts such as these, the results of Gabarino's study clearly reinforce the position of merit pay critics: extrinsic rewards produce an instrumental approach to teaching. Money is such a powerful influence on motivation that pay-for-performance may change the whole quality of education. Opponents of merit pay believe that teachers will "teach to the tests". **The content of teaching will, they assert, focus excessively on those criteria used to judge performance, and the form of teaching will be highly directive.** Low performing students may be put under too much pressure by teachers whose incomes partly depend on the students. Up to a point, the pressure may be beneficial, but the possibilities for excess and abuse are obvious. Even if no clear abuses occur, teaching will almost certainly give more emphasis to "quick fixes": **what** a solution is, not **how** to arrive at a solution. This is exactly the wrong direction in which to move education, merit pay opponents argue, because of the now rapid obsolescence of facts versus the continuing utility of methods.

If this line of reasoning is correct, then merit pay would do more than change teachers' attitudes toward teaching: **it would change the relationships between teachers and students.** Poor students would no longer pose challenges, they would pose threats. Teachers would have incentives to see that poor students are kept out of their classrooms, and they would have incentives to compete for better performers. Many parents, moreover, may be highly uncomfortable with merit pay once they realize what it could mean for a teacher's treatment of their child.

Incentives and Motivation

Opponents argue that **when teachers adopt an instrumental orientation toward their work and their students, their intrinsic motivation will diminish.** They believe there is a trade-off between the extrinsic and intrinsic rewards valued by teachers. Merit pay, they argue, will damage intrinsic motivation and produce costs in performance greater than any performance gains obtained from its introduction.

If the research summarized earlier is credited, then extrinsic rewards are likely to have negative effects on intrinsic motivation when a job involves a heavy measure of problem-solving and when neither solutions nor ways of producing them are readily apparent. Few occupations fit that description better than teaching. Problem-solving is a basic feature of many occupations but few, if any, make solutions so difficult to come by. Many features of teaching compel its practitioners to develop skills and standards of competence largely on their own, including:

- multiple, ambiguous, often conflicting outcomes, goals and criteria of assessment;
- the paucity of research on teaching (as opposed to learning) and the absence of any authoritative body of "how to" knowledge;
- the lack of a technical vocabulary which might facilitate the exchange of insights and the analysis of problems among colleagues; and,
- entry-processes, physical separation and time limitations which limit opportunities for such exchanges and analysis.

Teachers have few opportunities to step back from the concrete details of their classroom experience and to organize them into coherent patterns that might yield clear solutions. If there is a difference between the role requirements of teaching and the heuristic problem solving required of subjects in the experiments that have demonstrated the negative effects of extrinsic rewards, it is that the experimental subjects at least had the benefit of knowing what the problem was, even if they were not told how to solve it.

While these conditions make teaching onerous for some and frustrating for most, critics of merit pay claim they are also the conditions that motivate teacher performance. The key satisfaction obtained by teachers — the achievement that really urges them beyond simply meeting job requirements — is "reaching students" (Lortie, 1975). Of course they also work to meet economic needs, but what motivates them to **improve** their performance is the all too rare but intensely satisfying experience of educating minds. Opponents of merit pay assert that this type of motivation is a critical resource that our education system must not squander —and that merit pay would certainly do so, for all of the reasons cited by the "negative-effects" researchers. **If intrinsic motivation is driven out by an emphasis on pay-for-performance, the incentive to achieve high teacher performance will decline**.

But what of the argument that the **net** effect on performance could still be positive if additional motivation deriving from merit pay was greater than any loss in motivation deriving from decreased intrinsic motivation?

Merit pay critics point out that managers in the private sector, and scholars who have studied their experience, have come to realize that individual incentive pay will be successful only under particular conditions (for summaries see Lawler, 1977; Mahoney, 1979). The output produced by the individual employee must be easy to measure. Cooperation and teamwork among individual employees in the production process must not be important. Further, employees must not be forced to play a "zero-sum" compensation game in which one employee cannot earn significantly more without decreasing the amount of money that other employees can be paid. Employees, in other words, must be able to expand the pool of resources available for distribution as compensation. Sales people, for example, produce a product that is easily measured (gross or net sales), they often work individually rather than in teams, and on the basis of their own selling efforts they can increase the revenues of their employer (and thus their own incomes) without decreasing the earnings of the organization's other employees. The conditions that permit the successful use of incentive and bonus plans in sales occupations simply do not exist in teaching.

Incentive pay is also used in many industrial settings, where it takes the form of piece-rate payments. On the surface, the use of piece-rate systems might seem to require qualification of the arguments we just enumerated. Individual output is typically easy to measure, but often cooperation among employees is still important and individual production may have no direct effect on the amount of money available for distribution as incentive payments. But, in fact, piece-rate systems are often plagued with problems, and their problems stem directly from these factors. Labor-management bickering over the appropriate rates to be assigned different jobs is a constant feature of piece-rate systems, workers maintain constant surveillance of each other's production and are quick to discourage "rate-busters" who are likely to jeopardize other workers' earnings, and work groups are in a position to enforce informal limits on production in part because their members need each other's cooperation and informal job-knowledge to reach and maintain proficiency on their jobs (see Whyte, 1955). The saving grace of piece-rate systems is that a degree of friction and restriction on output are not fundamentally at odds with the employer's objectives, which are not to encourage more and more production but to stabilize and set a floor under production levels, thereby making unit labor costs more predictable. In teaching, where the objective is to promote continuous improvement in the quality of education, merit pay would be likely to generate all of the negative side-effects of piece-rate systems without producing corresponding benefits to the employer.

The discussion to this point has concentrated on possible disincentive effects among the group of "meritorious" teachers (presuming they are indentifiable). Additionallly, critics of merit pay believe that it may lower incentive among average teachers. The reason is more straightforward: **those who do not receive the merit increment will experience a relative decline in their rewards, and commensurately lower their performance**.

Impact on Working Relationships Among Teachers

There is the genuine danger — demonstrated by a considerable amount of experience — that **merit pay plans foster dissension, rivalry, and jealousy among teachers**. Several studies have documented increased conflict among faculty and the resentment of low-rated teachers (Casey, 1979). Weissman (1969) summarizes the situation:

> Merit pay rating, according to most studies, stimulates a competitive spirit (dissension, misunderstanding, suspicion, lowered morale) among teachers - a group which needs cooperation and a low pressure, high quality atmosphere to work best.

The key question is whether these problems are inevitable or can be overcome with sufficient planning and careful administration.

One aspect of this question concerns the **use of quotas** in a merit pay system. Advocates often concede that it is a mistake to use formal quotas to limit the number of merit increments, because of the dissension created. Merit pay critics, on other hand, maintain that the plans are inherently distributive and competitive, even if the limitations on the number of merit stipends are not as blatant as they are with a formal quota system. They are inherently competitive, critics argue, simply because the amount of money available for distribution to teachers is likely to be fixed. Unless a district has budgeted sufficient funds to give all its teachers the maximum stipend available, teachers will recognize that they are competing for a fixed and scarce number of increments.

There is a second, closely-related reason why critics claim merit pay generates competition, invidious comparisons, and lack of cooperation among teachers. Evaluators, they claim, are forced to compare one teacher with another when they make their ratings, even if they do not acknowledge that is what they are doing. Concepts such as "inferior", "average", and "outstanding" have no meaning apart from the group to which they are applied. Teachers recognize that higher-level administrators and boards of education will hold evaluators accountable for the ratings they produce. Since these higher level officials do not have the personal knowledge that allows them to challenge particular ratings, their basic criterion for judging an evaluator's performance will be whether he or she gives too many, too few, or "about the right number" of high, medium and low ratings. Evaluators, in turn, know that their judgments are likely to be challenged if they violate such expectations, but are likely to go unquestioned if they turn in a proper-looking distribution. Such informal pressures, sometimes supplemented by formal control mechanisms that require extra documentation for "high"ratings, make adversaries of fellow teachers, even if there are no formal quotas to proclaim the fact.

As noted earlier, these two conditions — scarce increments and interpersonal standards of assessment — make merit pay in teaching quite different from pay-for-performance systems in sales occupations and in certain entrepreneurial professions, where employees are individually responsible for bringing new money into their organizations. There may be a measure of competition among employees in such settings, but they are not competing for the same (fixed) sum of money and the amount of money they do generate is itself the basic standard of assessment: absolute performance, not relative performance, determines the size of an individual's rewards. In teaching, where the individual teacher's performance has no bearing on the amount of money available to be distributed as rewards, the standards of assessment are necessarily relative and interpersonal.

The **issue of secrecy** poses similar problems. A number of studies have documented that, when merit pay ratings are public knowledge, those not designated as meritorious can suffer the embarassment of having parents ask that children be reassigned out of their classes to those of "superior" teachers (Weissman, 1969; Conte and Mason, 1972). Advocates of merit pay often acknowledge this problem and some advocates recommend that ratings and merit increments be kept confidential. Critics and other advocates point out, however, that maintaining strict secrecy only leaves a void that is invariably filled with rumors, misperceptions, and distorted information, all of which serve to undermine the atmosphere of confidence, respect, honesty, and trust which are vital to the program's success.

For these reasons, critics believe that merit pay **necessarily** generates poor working relationships among teachers. Sloppy design or poor administration may aggravate the problems, but refinements and better administration of the plans will not remove them. The problems are inherent in the basic concept itself, they claim.

Impact on Teacher-Administrator Relationships

Whatever the strengths or weaknesses of particular arguments over merit pay, it is difficult to avoid drawing one conclusion: the basic purpose of any merit pay scheme is to supplement what is perceived to be the insufficient professional commitment of some teachers by adding inducements formulated and controlled by someone else. The basic purpose of merit pay is manipulative and **reflective of distrust** in a generally-unspecified number of teachers, no matter how carefully school boards or administrators avoid publicizing that fact. If that characterization of merit pay is accepted, then the frictions between administrators and teachers often associated with merit pay are not simply reflections of technical problems, even if the specific issues that seem to generate such conflicts might be framed in those terms.

Friction and lack of acceptance of merit pay could have far-reaching consequences, even in unorganized districts. Creating an atmosphere of conflict between a teaching staff and administration or within the teaching staff itself is clearly undesirable. Implementation of a compensation system that teachers find offensive, because they either disagree with its underlying principles or dislike its administrative aspects, could produce just such an atmosphere. The quality of education will almost certainly suffer in a school filled with bitter and resentful teachers.

There is a more specific reason, however, for thinking that merit pay will damage the relationships between administrators and their staffs. Research on school effectiveness makes it clear that the leadership provided by a principal to his or her staff is critical to a school's performance. Research also indicates that principals in effective schools pay special attention to monitoring all that goes on in their buildings. They pay careful attention to the design and maintenance of formal evaluation procedures, but they recognize that evaluation and monitoring cannot be confined to formal procedures. Rather, they treat evaluation and monitoring as on-going processes that occur wherever teachers and administrators exchange and assess information (Little, 1982; Leithwood and Montgomery, 1982). There is little doubt that these observations are all closely connected. Information is a critical resource to teachers and to administrators, but it can easily get buried in the highly compartmentalized structure of a school. One of the reasons a principal is so critical to school effectiveness is that he or she serves as a focal point — sometimes the only focal point — for gathering, analyzing, and disseminating information within a building.

A principal obtains most of his or her information from teachers. The circumstances of principals differ here from the conditions faced by managers in most other occupational settings, because most managers have independent and timely access to data on such things as sales, production levels, and error rates. If teachers do not **volunteer** information to their principal about problems they are confronting, a principal may never become aware of those difficulties or may learn of them only when situations are out of control. **Merit pay gives teachers a strong incentive not to bring problems to their principal's attention and to be selective about the information they do provide to a principal.** Nothing could more fundamentally weaken the principal's leadership role.

The issue is not whether school administrators should accede to the demands of a teaching staff full of prima donnas. Rather, the issue is whether a particular compensation system promotes a harmonious environment in which teachers and administrators can work effectively, or whether it instead results in a conflictual environment in which the two groups see each other as adversaries and in which neither can perform up to its potential.

Impact on Parent-School Relations

As noted above, with a merit pay system, principals may be plagued with parents wanting to switch their children into classes taught by "meritorious" teachers. This type of problem already exists in many school districts, even without merit pay, but it is almost certain to be magnified when a district officially designates some teachers as more meritorious than others. Administrators may try to maintain strict secrecy concerning merit ratings, but information probably will leak out or else rumors will develop. For these reasons, and because secrecy destroys merit pay's usefulness as a means of providing public recognition and examples of model teachers, many principals prefer to make the increments public. In short, merit pay is likely to be accompanied by conflict between schools and parents (and also conflict among parents) over the assignment of children to classes taught by particular teachers.

Judgmental versus Diagnostic Feedback

Research indicates that effective schools use their evaluation and monitoring systems to identify both weaknesses which need to be corrected and strengths which can be capitalized upon (Wynne, 1981; Little, 1982). They use them, in other words, as **diagnostic instruments**, rather than as instruments designed to produce generalizations about the overall performance of individual teachers. In one formulation, the distinction has been made between "summative" and "formative" evaluations. The former is an overall, positive or negative judgment; the latter analyzes the elements of performance, without an overall pro or con assessment. One researcher illustrates the importance of such a distinction: those responsible for evaluation and monitoring systems in effective schools, she notes, appear to make special efforts to avoid casting **blame** for the problems they identify. Their purpose is to find **reasons** for the strengths and weaknesses they identify, and they treat teachers as equals in exploring solutions. That is, they use formative evaluations. This researcher goes on to point out that there is a fine line between "finding fault" and "finding reasons", but that is all the more reason why the distinction needs to be made (Little, 1982).

Merit evaluations are summative, and attempts to accompany the system with formative evaluations will almost certainly end in failure. The two are contradictory. Merit evaluators may not fault teachers for everything that goes wrong in the classroom, but their job is to look for things that **are** their fault. Teachers know that this is the case, and that knowledge is likely to have a fundamental effect on how they approach the evaluation process. However nice or well-meaning or "objective" an evaluator appears, he or she is decisive in whether the teacher obtains a pay raise. As we noted above, at the very least the teacher has an incentive not to volunteer any information that might be construed as a sign of personal ineffectiveness. At worst, he or she has an incentive to distort the information that is available to the evaluator.

Impact on Staff Development

In effective schools, teachers freely exchange and share information (Little, 1982). They discuss their mutual problems, analyze each other's teaching techniques, and help each other out. In this way, teachers receive a considerable amount of informal training from each other. Critics of merit pay claim that it will undermine the openness and exchange of information among teachers. Under a merit pay plan, teachers who help colleagues to become more effective in the classroom may be taking money out of their own pockets. As stated previously, critics argue that merit pay fosters competition among teachers, rather than cooperation in becoming a better team of educators.

Further, several of the studies of effective schools indicate that formal in-service training works best when teachers play an active role in designing the training themselves; i.e., if they gear the programs to the specific problems which they share in common (Griffin, 1982;

Wood, McQuarrie and Thompson, 1982). Merit pay may not prevent such efforts, but it will certainly weaken them if it provides incentives for teachers either to hide their problems or to see each other as competitive threats.

Measuring Performance

Merit pay depends on measuring performance. Even if the motivation arguments for merit pay are supportable, they are irrelevant if merit cannot be measured validly and reliably. An evaluation system is valid if it measures what it is supposed to be measuring, and is reliable if the measurement instrument produces consistent measures. For example, if a person truly weighs 180 pounds, and a scale consistently records his or her weight as 170, the scale is not a valid measure, although it is reliable. On the other hand, an instrument that is unreliable is necessarily also invalid.

Old Style merit pay assesses teacher performance in the classroom. Methods vary, but they generally focus on a teacher's presentation style and how he or she organizes the content of lessons. For instance, a criterion may be a teacher's ability to present material orally in a clear and understandable voice. To evaluate a teacher on this factor, a school district must rely on principals or others who periodically take "samples" of the teacher's performance by visiting the classroom. Given that a merit pay system requires that all teachers be observed, and not just those who are known to be having difficulties, critics claim that administrators invariably lack the time to observe each teacher often enough to form an accurate estimate of his or her overall performance on any particular criterion.

Even if this hurdle could be overcome, such estimates necessarily involve subjective judgments. For example, if a particular teacher repeats a point several times, in a slightly different way each time, is that a sign that he or she is particularly careful about making points clear, or is it a sign of an inability to make the point clear the first time? Do the evaluator's perceptions of clarity accurately reflect what is and is not clear to a teacher's students? What if a complex point is unclear to an outside observer because it has been stated cryptically, whereas it is perfectly clear to students because they have heard it stated more carefully and slowly many times before? Again, has the observer visited the teacher's classroom often enough to recognize such situations? As troublesome as these questions are, they are the simplest to deal with.

If the clarity of oral presentations is the task evaluated, it is assumed that the ability to perform the task in a superior fashion is related to the quality of the education the teacher is providing his or her students. But it is obviously difficult to single out one specific teacher task or behavior that may be responsible for high student achievement. Most evaluation systems, therefore, will use several criteria to assess performance.

Multiple criteria only multiply the problems. Can an observer be sufficiently discriminating on any particular criterion when he or she must be looking for evidence of a teacher's performance on many dimensions at once? How should performance on two different criteria be evaluated, if the two criteria (say, maintenance of classroom order and sensitivity to the needs of individual students) place contradictory demands on a teacher in a particular situation? Most people would be prepared to accept both of those criteria as appropriate considerations in judging teaching effectiveness, but an evaluation scheme that must generate overall ratings of effectiveness, based on individual factor ratings, cannot properly reflect the need to make compromises between different criteria of effectiveness. Evaluators who are sensitive to such considerations can and almost certainly do make allowances for such contradictory pressures, but in doing so, they introduce a further measure of subjectivity into the rating process.

The problem of validity gets even more complicated when the evaluations of other teachers are taken into account. Is it appropriate to use the same rating factors to evaluate the performance of a kindergarten teacher, a middle school special education teacher, and a high school physics teacher? If the same overall benchmark ratings will be used to determine the salaries of each of them, is it fair not to use the same factors? What weights should different factors receive? On what basis can a district justify giving equal or different weights to different factors? Again, is it appropriate to use the same weights for factors that may vary in importance from one type of classroom to another? Is it fair not to do so?

Critics claim that to avoid these problems districts are compelled to adopt evaluation criteria that are exceptionally broad and general. These "lowest common denominators", they argue, not only render the evaluation process all the more subjective and ineffective as diagnostic instruments, they also make a mockery of claims that merit pay evaluations are meant to make teachers sensitive to demands for excellence. Their effect is to divert attention from the careful scrutiny of specific situations, which is the approach actually needed to help teachers improve their performance.

The identity and organizational position of evaluators are also major concerns. Teachers may object to being rated only by administrators (Knox, 1970), since administrators may not be sensitive enough to matters of teaching technique. Administrators may have been away from classroom teaching for many years and may have left because they did not find their skills well-suited to the classroom. For these and other reasons, critics claim that administrators may not be qualified to recognize effective teaching. This criticism reinforces the previous arguments about the validity of old-style evaluation procedures and makes subjectivity an all-the-more sensitive issue. It also raises the issue of reliability.

The difficulty of obtaining reliable measures of teacher performance based on classroom visitations is well known. It is impossible to erase all bias in a rating based upon classroom observation: the individual rater cannot help but be somewhat subjective. Reliability is not simply a function of the good will of the evaluator, however. It is not necessary for a rater to discriminate maliciously against a teacher or to slant an observation report intentionally for evaluation measures to be unreliable, although of course there is the opportunity for raters to do so. Even raters with the best of intentions may be incapable of making reliable evaluations.

The root cause of unreliable measures is the difficulty of defining superior teaching. For example, in an experiment cited by McDowell (1973), a group of 65 principals evaluated a first grade teacher during a training program. The principals' ratings of the teacher ranged from "exceptional" to "doubtful". Moreover, principals classified as experienced varied as much in their ratings as those who were inexperienced. McDowell concludes: "In the face of this kind of report, it is little wonder that teachers greet merit rating proposals with considerable skepticism".

New Style merit pay attempts to side-step these objections by rewarding teachers on the basis of output measures like student performance on standardized tests. In Houston, for example, teachers in a school are rewarded if student achievement test scores surpass a projected goal. The system has "face validity" in that the goals themselves become the system's operational definition of teaching excellence. But what exactly is being rewarded under such a system? In this case it is not specific classroom tasks and behaviors. Teachers are informed, by means of an increase in pay, that they have done something right and ought to continue doing it. They may have only vague notions, however, of what specific behavioral or pedagogical approaches have resulted in the improvement of test scores. Generally, no attempt is made under New Style merit plans to link particular teacher tasks to an increase in student achievement. Indeed, in Houston the aggregation of test scores to the level of the school compounds the problem. If the test scores in a particular school improve, all teachers are rewarded, even though an individual teacher in the school may be engaging in behavior that actually is stifling the education of his or her students. Is this really measuring performance?

The problem is even more apparent for teachers or schools that fail to achieve pre-established goals. Assuming the goals themselves were not set unrealistically high — and there is no way of independently evaluating that possibility — there is the built-in assumption that teachers are responsible for their students' failure to meet the test score targets: that teachers either have done something wrong or have failed to do something they should have been doing and that it is up to them to discover how to remedy the situation.

In fact, many other reasons beyond an individual teacher's performance may be responsible. For example, the academic ability of students assigned to a class can vary markedly from year to year, a district's curriculum may change, a teacher may be assigned additional duties or have less support staff. All these can affect test scores. In other words, external factors that influence test scores can render unreliable the New Style performance measures. Jackson (1968), in a study of teachers who had been identified by their principals as "outstanding", reports that such teachers tend to dismiss the usefulness of standardized test scores as a means of assessing their own performance. Teacher opposition and general dissatisfaction with evaluations are the reasons most often given by districts for abandoning merit pay. The two reasons, moreover, are closely connected. Perceptions that merit evaluations are biased, subjective, and generally unfair are probably more responsible for teacher opposition to merit pay systems than any other factor.

Advocates of merit pay generally acknowledge that teacher confidence in a merit pay plan is essential to a plan's success, and they recognize that weaknesses in an evaluation system are often what destroys such confidence. They insist, however, that the problems are technical and can be overcome with sufficient care in planning and administration (see Educational Research Service, 1979). Critics of merit pay, on the other hand, maintain that the problems of validity, reliability, subjectivity, and lack of teacher confidence reflect a fundamental weakness in the assumption that teacher effectiveness can be identified, measured and summarized in objective ratings. There is strong reason to believe that generality and subjectivity in merit evaluations (which are cited by merit pay advocates as "technical" problems) are present because there are equally if not more serious problems with seemingly-objective measures of performance. The critics believe that the concept of measuring merit has fundamental flaws: the problems are not "technical," they are inherent.

In the context of merit pay, the method of assessment must be accurate enough to justify deciding people's incomes on the basis of the results. This is a harsh spotlight to put on any evaluation measure. There is no doubt that principals and others have informed opinions about who is and who is not a good teacher. And often the opinions will be well justified. It is a big step, however, to base teachers' salary levels on these judgments — and to have to justify the assessments in the eyes of the teachers.

Teacher Recruitment

The process of deciding on an occupation is long and complex. It depends heavily on intangible factors: parental role models, childhood experiences with the people in various occupations, and so on. Salary is just one part of the decision, and a potential increment for excellent performance is even more marginal. Still, salary is certainly one influence.

Studies indicate that once people have narrowed down their occupation choices to possibilities that seem reasonably attractive, their attention will focus on entry-level salary, income security and probable lifetime earnings. New teachers are unlikely to receive merit increments, thus perceived entry-level salaries probably would not be affected by merit pay. As for income security and career earnings, they can be captured in the concept of the **present value** of future earnings. Present value is the value in today's dollars of a projected income stream. The present value of a projected income stream is lowered if the **uncertainty** of that income stream is increased.

Merit pay would increase the uncertainty of teachers' career earnings. Highly optimistic potential recruits will not be deterred, but **taking the group of potential recruits as a whole, raising uncertainty will lower the present value of teacher career earnings**. Moreover, with the current type of compensation system, teaching has a clear income advantage among other occupations in the same salary range: it has comparatively high income security. Merit pay would remove or endanger that advantage.

Teacher Turnover

Critics of merit pay assert that **retention of teachers in the profession is likely to be harmed by the work relations, extrinsic motivation, and instrumental attitudes engendered by merit pay**. On the other hand, concern over salary is one reason why some teachers change occupations, and to the extent that merit pay raises salaries then fewer will leave. The net outcome, then, depends on the relative strength of these two effects.

In general, employees pass through two distinctive phases in deciding to resign from an organization. The first entails the decison to **consider** resignation; the second concerns the subsequent process of deciding whether to **actually** leave. Most turnover occurs during the first few years in an occupation; the rate then drops off dramatically. The direct costs of changing employment and (perhaps) one's residence, the indirect costs of losing salary credits for years of experience and employer pension contributions, and plain inertia discourage thoughts of leaving after a few years of employment with any given employer.

After the first few years, thoughts of resignation are largely prompted by work activity **in itself** rather than by relative salary and benefit levels. Now, this generalization only holds within a certain range: if salary differences in accessible occupations become "too" large then people will take notice. The relative pay levels of most occupations rarely shift dramatically, however, thus for most practical purposes the key to the resignation rate of experienced professionals lies in the intrinsic rewards they obtain from their jobs. In short, most experienced teachers, especially the most dedicated teachers, will only consider leaving if they no longer gain sufficient intrinsic satisfactions from the profession.

Merit pay, as noted previously, may lower intrinsic rewards. It may discourage autonomy and independent problem-solving. Teachers may be less able to focus on intangibles such as "reaching" students. Additionally, merit pay is likely to raise the level of conflict and dissension. **These changes in the process of teaching itself could lead many teachers to consider alternative occupations.**

Once this point is reached, then the factors addressed by merit pay (extrinsic rewards) come into play. A higher salary grade derived from merit pay may, in this phase, lower the likelihood of resignation. Teacher salaries, however, are low relative to other professions, and any merit increments would have to be quite large to make up the difference. The possibility of merit pay lowering the likelihood of resignation, moreover, would only apply to those who obtain or are likely to obtain merit stipends; the system would only make those who do not get stipends more conscious of their relative salary deprivation. If a district observes a policy of giving stipends to all but its poorest teachers, the effects of this consideration might well be positive: some poor teachers might decide to leave. But if a district reserves its stipends for teachers who are considered to be outstanding — which is the only logical approach to take if the point is to emphasize excellence in teaching — then the teachers who are most likely to be discouraged and to consider leaving are those who would have some reason to believe they **might** have received stipends: those who have received average ratings and think (correctly or incorrectly) that they deserve above average ratings.

Once an experienced teacher reaches the stage of seriously evaluating the returns from other occupations, the likelihood of resignation is probably high. The best way to avoid unwanted teacher resignations is to lower the probability that a teacher will begin looking seriously at alternatives. Teachers, like most employees in other intrinsically rewarding occupations, will not scan other options while their job satisfaction is high. Above a minimal salary level, job satisfaction in large part depends on rewards found within the work process itself. Principals should do all they can to not endanger that source of satisfaction — and opponents of merit pay claim that it would do precisely that.

Administrative Burden

Merit pay systems are administratively complex and cumbersome. In Old Style systems, in particular, much of the complexity is due to the need to measure teacher performance on a regular and continuing basis. If a plan calls for in-class evaluation, its authors must decide who will perform evaluations, at what time intervals they should be carried out, the means used to report the evaluations, and what kind of evaluation criteria and forms or checklists will be used. Unlike evaluation for tenure review or teacher development, the system necessarily involves thorough and periodic assessments of all teachers in a district.

To illustrate these general points, we list below a number of prescriptions that one management consulting organization suggests must be followed in designing and administering a merit pay plan. The consulting organization is frequently a champion of merit pay for teachers. Each prescription illustrates a different element of administrative complexity in the well-administered merit pay plan. (Omitted are references to a number of other studies, from which these recommendations are drawn.)

> 1) Careful advance planning, researching likely pitfalls and tailoring the plan to the district's specified situation;
> 2) Continuous reevaluation of the plan itself;
> 3) Detailed explanations to existing and new teachers of how the plan will operate;
> 4) Thorough training of evaluators and analysis of their experience, to catch and correct specific problems;
> 5) Continuous evaluation and reevaluation of all teachers, using teams rather than single evaluators to avoid problems of subjectivity;
> 6) Follow-up conferences with all teachers;
> 7) Provision for an appeals procedure by which

teachers can question, challenge, and seek modifications of their ratings (Educational Research
Service, 1979).

Even if these points are framed as technical issues and not as
fundamental problems, they indicate why many districts have found
merit pay programs to be administratively burdensome.

Overall Costs

The administrative burden of merit pay illustrates one reason why
**the monetary costs of a merit pay system will almost certainly be
steep.** McDowell (1973) reports that one merit pay plan had
administrative overhead costs that amounted to an extra 18 percent
of personnel costs. Although similar data for other plans are not
available, the Educational Research Service (1979) cites that figure
as if it might be typical of other plans as well.

It is more difficult to generalize about the costs of the merit
increments themselves. Additional salary costs could be limited by
restricting the size of individual increments, by constraining the
number of increments granted, or by cutting back on the base
salaries to which increments are added, but even the most enthusiastic
advocates of merit pay warn against such measures. If the sums
allotted for individual increments are restricted, the stipends will be
too small to be effective as either rewards or incentives. If the
number of available stipends is constrained, either directly by
imposition of a quota or indirectly by tight eligibility standards, the
program will almost certainly foster ill-will and unhealthy competition
among teachers. It will also generate the perception that evaluation
standards are being manipulated for budgetary reasons. If a district
tries to save money by cutting back on base salaries, it will make the
manipulative character of the program all-too-apparent to its existing
teachers and will put the district at a disadvantage in recruiting new
teachers and retaining existing ones. A district's base salaries must
remain competitive, in other words, if it is to have any hope of
convincing teachers that the program is a genuine effort to reward
excellence and not a cynical attempt to save money (McKenna,
1973; Educational Research Service, 1979).

Critics contend that budgetary pressures, being specific and immediate, invariably take precedence over the poorly-defined need to fund a merit pay program "adequately", forcing all three types of compromises noted above. Even if it is not the case when a plan is first implemented, the possibility grows more likely over time, as the enthusiasm that first generated the program begins to dissipate and its administrative and monetary costs become more apparent. Regardless of the steps that a district might take to limit the indirect and direct costs of a merit pay plan, however, all available evidence suggests that such a plan still will cost significantly more than the unified salary schedule it is designed to replace.

Collective Bargaining Issues

Teacher unions almost invariably oppose the introduction of a merit pay system in a school district. Officially, both the National Education Association and the American Federation of Teachers are on record as being willing to "consider" some modifications to the unified schedule, but their opposition to merit pay, at least as it is usually presented, is long-standing and widely-recognized. Advocates of merit pay, in fact, often claim that the **only** real opposition to the concept comes from union leaders and that this opposition does not reflect the attitudes of teachers themselves. No surveys that we know of actually document this assertion, but there are certainly teachers at all points on the spectrum of attitudes to merit pay.

Unions are political organizations that, by necessity and often by law, are required to represent and be sensitive to the interests of all their constituents. Their leaders' perspectives on issues such as merit pay are bound to be somewhat different from those of individual teachers, if only because they have to focus on how such systems will affect teachers as a group whereas individual teachers are more likely to take a narrower perspective. Union leaders, after all, cannot help but recognize that only a certain proportion of their constituents will be awarded merit stipends, while individual teachers may well assume that they are likely to be one of the persons thus honored.

As political leaders, subject to elections and responsible for the well-being of the organization as a whole, union officials have special reasons to be concerned about the competition and divisiveness that merit pay can generate among teachers. With merit pay, they face the problems of negotiating and policing safeguards against favoritism and abuse: problems that individual teachers can ignore if they choose to do so. Union leaders, moreover, recognize that whatever funds are allocated to a merit pay program will not be available for base salary increases — and that they are not likely to get much credit for the former, particularly if a large proportion of those funds are directed to overhead expenses and not to teacher stipends themselves.

It would be a mistake to dismiss the opposition of teacher unions simply because their leaders' perspectives may differ somewhat from those held by their rank and file members. Unions have "institutional memories" — their positions on many issues are influenced by knowledge of how similar issues have been dealt with in the past — which means that their leaders' **current** positions may be more accurate predictors of teachers' **future** attitudes than the attitudes of teachers themselves. In a sense, moreover, the considerations that influence union leaders' perspectives more nearly match the considerations that influence school boards and administrators than those that influence individual teachers: union leaders, board members and administrators must all be concerned with the overall effects of a compensation system on teachers and the school system as a whole. Union opposition, from this point of view, is a healthy reminder to board members and administrators that they cannot afford to assess the benefits of merit pay solely in terms of how it might affect those teachers who obtain merit stipends.

It also would be a mistake to assume that there is a large gap between the attitudes of union leaders and their consitituents. The fact that unions are political organizations — and the fact that, in teaching, the union leaders who have direct responsibility for bargaining policy are teachers themselves, with day-to-day contact with other teachers — guarantee a measure of responsiveness to member attitudes. The problems that most concern teachers are those to which their union leaders have to be most sensitive. From this perspective, union opposition to merit pay should be considered a reflection of other, more underlying issues: issues that school districts would be well-advised to recognize and deal with **before** rather than **after** they decide to implement merit pay.

School board members and administrators should be aware that, if problems arise with merit pay, teachers will probably turn to their unions for help. As one participant in a union conference pointed out recently, the one saving grace about merit pay — from the point of view of union leaders — is that it might be a full employment act for union representatives. Lest that comment be passed off as idle speculation, Doremus (1982) reports that one of the only lasting effects of the once-touted Kalamazoo, Michigan accountability and merit pay plans, initiated and then abandoned in the 1970's, was mobilization of teacher support for union involvement in school board elections.

Weighing the Theoretical Arguments Against Actual Experience with Merit Plans

The theoretical advantages and disadvantages of merit pay could be debated indefinitely, but the acid test lies in its implementation. Advocates can try to explain past failures by pointing to "technical" errors (which might be removable through more careful efforts or more resources), but the track record of merit pay must contain some lessons. The historical experience is very discouraging. The majority fail within a few years. One survey of school district experience with merit pay, for example, found that 10.5 percent of all school districts surveyed either had a merit pay plan in 1977-78 or else had had such a plan at some time in the past. Of these, roughly 61.4 percent had dropped the plan and returned to the single salary schedule, after an average of six years experience. Of the remainder, over half were still within this six-year trial period, indicating that many of them were probably candidates for disillusionment as well (Educational Research Service, 1979).

An early study (Davis, 1961) summarized reasons why 49 school systems (in cities of 30,000 or more population) discontinued merit pay programs over the 1938-39 to 1959-60 period. Unsatisfactory evaluation systems and teacher dissension were the major reasons for ending the merit schemes. Schools found it too difficult to decide who deserved merit increments, and subjectivity, inconsistency and partiality plagued the programs. Teachers too frequently saw the merit pay plan as unfair, and it created distrust, resentment, and conflict both among teachers and between teachers and administrators. Districts were often forced to alleviate these consequences by spreading merit increments wider and wider, until the payments no longer distinquished between excellent and average teachers. School systems also noted that the merit schemes were an excessive administrative burden, were too costly, and placed unacceptable loads on those responsible for teacher ratings.

A more recent study (Educational Research Service, 1979) of 239 school systems with enrollments of 300 or more found similar reasons for discontinuing merit pay. Forty percent had administrative problems, especially difficulties with obtaining consistent and objective performance evaluation. Thirty-one percent also cited teacher opposition, destroyed morale, and severe dissension. Teachers negotiated the plan out of the contract in about 17% of the cases, and a similar proportion dropped the program because of financial problems: the plans were too costly or the merit increments possible under their budgets were too small to be effective as incentives.

Experience is never an indisputable guide. Circumstances and methods change, voiding lessons drawn from apparently similar events in the past. Are the merit pay plans proposed and the circumstances surrounding them substantially different from those previously attempted? Generalization is especially difficult here, but the evidence of past failure must at least put the onus of proof on the shoulders of merit pay advocates. Based on the past, a reasonable presumption is that merit pay plans will fail. Consequently, proponents should show evidence to the contrary if their plans are to be accepted.

Merit pay has major weaknesses, but what are the alternatives? Merit pay has received so much attention in large part because too many observers are unaware of other means of raising teaching standards. The **desire for change** in current education — virtually any change — is driving much of the support for merit pay, simply because those concerned have little information about alternative avenues for change.

The remainder of this monograph discusses alternatives to merit pay. The discussion is divided into several sections. The first discusses the most obvious: sticking with the existing system. Another discusses relatively minor modifications that might strengthen the existing system without fundamental change. The next discusses more controversial changes that could be implemented as temporary exceptions to the unified system, leaving its basic structure intact. The next-to-last section discusses several proposals structured around the concept of a "career ladder," and the final section discusses even more fundamental changes in how our schools are managed.

Alternatives: Retaining the Unified Salary Schedule

The unified schedule has literally stood the test of time. The survival of the unified salary schedule for over half a century is not in itself proof that the system should continue, but it does suggest strongly that the system should not be discarded without very compelling reasons. Moreover, if there is one clear lesson from the social change efforts of the last two decades, it is that the attempts often backfire. Unintended consequences are the rule rather than the exception. This too is not an argument for maintaining the status quo; it is, however, an argument for humility. Social scientists' theories and research provide valuable insights, but societies and their organizations are so extraordinarily complex that modelling problems, solutions, and outcomes is extremely difficult. Clearly, if we see a fault, we should consider ways of remedying it — if education standards are too low, reform should be attempted. But ideas about how the world works should be applied cautiously when they challenge practices that have been developed incrementally over a long period and through the experiences of many people. At the very least, the continuing pre-eminence of the unified salary schedule demands an assessment of why it has been so popular.

From the viewpoint of achieving high quality education, the system has two basic strengths:

- it reflects our basic understanding of how teachers acquire their skills; and
- it is a system of compensation that has minimal impact on **other** school processes.

As to the first of these, broad surveys and in-depth studies repeatedly tell us that teachers learn how to teach by **being** teachers — by confronting and resolving for themselves the practical problems of managing a classroom. Schools of education do a relatively good job of giving would-be teachers the substantive knowledge they will need when they enter a classroom; they also provide insights into how individual children learn. But substantive knowledge and learning theory do not teach someone how to **teach**. They do not teach someone how to "read" a classroom full of youngsters or how best to organize and manage the literally hundreds of interactions that occur in a single classroom in a single day.

Practice teaching exposes education majors to some of the practical problems they can expect to face, and teachers usually rate their relatively-brief period of practice teaching to be the single most important part of their formal college education. Such ratings, however, say more about the inadequacy of "outside" training and the importance of direct classroom experience than they do about the adequacy of practice teaching itself. The practical techniques, analytic skills, and intuition that teachers need to be effective in the classroom are acquired in the classroom. If experience is the single most important ingredient in learning how to teach, then it is both logical and equitable that a compensation system should reward additional experience with additional pay.

The second basic strength of the unified salary schedule is that, unlike merit pay, it does not inhibit the use of other mechanisms that raise teacher performance. For example:

- It does not encourage administrators to water down their expectations of teachers, to focus attention on lowest common denominators, or to evaluate only those aspects of teaching that are easily measured;
- It does not give teachers incentive to perceive high expectations as threats to their income security or to keep problems and potentially negative information from coming to the attention of their principals;
- It does not pit the interests of one teacher against those of others, inhibiting joint problem-solving and the exchange of job-knowledge among teachers; and
- Perhaps most importantly, it does not give teachers reasons to think their students stand between them and a raise in pay: teachers can try innovative techniques and concentrate on securing intrinsic satisfaction from the process of teaching itself, knowing that the greatest rewards often come from finding new ways of reaching their poorest students; administrators can assign teachers to classrooms and pupils to teachers without incurring charges that they are prejudicing some teachers' chances for a pay raise when they make such assignments.

Far from discouraging innovation or forcing administrators to treat all teachers alike, as some critics claim, the unified salary schedule actually allows for more innovation, critical judgment, and administrative flexibility than any compensation system that explicitly links salary determinations to assessments of performance.

This backhanded way of characterizing the strengths of the unified salary schedule also indicates the limitations of the system. Apart from the incentive to obtain further education, which often prompts increased self-evaluation of performance as well as providing substantive knowledge, the unified salary schedules does little to **directly promote** quality teaching and better schools. It does not prevent administrators and teachers from promoting those objectives, but it also does not help them.

Furthermore, saying that experience is needed to be an effective teacher is not equivalent to saying that teaching skills necessarily continue to improve over the whole of a career. Teachers may stop looking for better approaches once they develop classroom methods that satisfy their own individual criteria. Physical separation, time limitations, and a variety of other factors tend to isolate the individual teacher from peers and administrators, limiting his or her exposure to new ideas. Also, the advantages of tying salary to experience and education do not directly address the argument that school effectiveness is more than a matter of individual skills. Teachers' collective efforts can suffer, regardless of their individual skills, and the unified salary schedule is little help in this respect.

Research on compensation administration indicates the difficulties of employing compensation systems to simultaneously work toward multiple goals. Compensation systems are powerful but unwieldy tools. Unintended consequences are rife. While merit pay has some advantages, it would probably aggravate many of the motivation and coordination problems it is intended to solve. Still, teaching as an occupation and schools as organizations do have some of the problems that advocates of merit pay have identified. The advocates are correct when they argue that the present compensation system does little positive to help us overcome these problems.

While teachers unions are probably right when they claim that the most important thing we could do about compensation would be to raise teachers' salaries, the advocates of merit pay are probably also right when they claim that the public will not pay for salary increases unless convinced that the expenditures will have a direct and positive effect on the quality of education. There are reasons to be cautious when we look for ways to reform the current teacher compensation system, but there are powerful reasons to look.

Alternatives: Reforms Within the Unified Salary Schedule

Several modifications could be made to the present teacher compensation system without changing its basic structure. Some would be more controversial than others; some are already incorporated in the salary schedules of several districts.

Consolidating Increments

There are good reasons for many districts to consider **consolidating steps on existing schedules,** to provide fewer but larger increments for experience and (perhaps) educational credits. At present, the average experience step yields a four percent increase in salary; the average increment for education (based on 15 credit hours) yields a five percent increase. Research evidence suggests that such small increments are barely noticeable to employees, particularly if they coincide with cost-of-living or other general increases that typically go into effect at the beginning of the school year. If they are barely noticeable, teachers are unlikely to think of them as a significant reward. Consolidating steps would not be easy — initially some teachers would have to be given larger increases than others — but phasing in a new, consolidated schedule over several years, and coupling it with general increases for all teachers, would help overcome obstacles.

Increase the Overall Rewards for Experience

With or without consolidation, there are good reasons to **substantially increase the size of increments,** particularly those associated with years of experience. On average, a teacher with a bachelor's degree who enters at step 1 of a salary schedule and anticipates reaching the schedule maximum can expect a total increase for experience of only 50-55 percent; even if he or she also expects to accumulate education credits and reach, say, the maximum for an MA plus 15 credit hours, he or she can expect only about an 85 percent total increase in salary over the course of his or her career. Most other occupations allow employees to make much more significant salary gains over their careers. These comparisons make it all the more likely that the salary compression in teaching will have serious effects on pay-satisfaction, turnover, and recruitment of new teachers.

Restrictions on Credited Courses

Many districts already **limit the kinds of outside courses that are given salary credit,** to provide some assurance that the district will actually benefit from the courses a teacher takes. The most common limitation is one that specifies that the courses must fall within the teacher's existing area of concentration or certification. Sometimes there is also provision for crediting course work that would lead to new certification in an area of existing or anticipated teacher shortages.

Salary Credits for In-Service Education

Districts also might **grant salary credits for in-service education,** taking corresponding steps to upgrade the quality and length of courses they offer. Such courses can be tailored to a district's specific needs, and they can provide teachers with opportunities to discuss common problems and strengthen their collegial ties. If teachers are responsible for planning and teaching courses themselves, then such courses can also be a way of involving teachers in the analysis of district needs and a way of recognizing and tapping the special skills and competencies of particular teachers.

Pay for Retraining in Shortage Subject Areas

A third way of using education credits to strengthen a district's educational programs — one that might help ease shortages in hard-to-fill subject matter areas — would be for districts and/or states to **pay the full cost of outside courses in areas of critical teacher shortages.** Teachers in other subject matter areas would be encouraged to seek certification in hard-to-fill areas, and teachers already certified in those areas would have incentives to remain in a district — incentives that are likely to be more acceptable to other teachers than the direct salary differentials some observers have recommended.

Alternatives: Making Exceptions to the Unified Salary Schedule

The alternative approaches discussed in the previous section would require no modification of the unified salary schedule at all; they represent ways in which school districts might use the existing system to better advantage. The alternatives to be discussed in later sections would represent significant departures from current compensaton or managerial practices in public education, although parts of them might be adopted without modifying the unified schedule. The alternatives to be discussed in this section do not fall clearly in either category; they would represent significant changes, but they would be framed as **limited exceptions** to the existing system.

The authors do not endorse any of the approaches to be discussed in this section. All three approaches have attractive features, but their negative features probably outweigh their positive ones. Readers are entitled to draw their own conclusions, however, and the authors believe that a **better** case can be made for these proposals than for most of the wholesale revisions to the unified salary schedule often discussed. In fact, each of these approaches represents a variation on a more sweeping proposal. Each is framed as a limited exception to the unified schedule in order to indicate that **if** such proposals are to be considered there are at least ways of minimizing their negative effects and maximizing the chances that they might do some good. The first approach is a variation on what was earlier called "speciality-linked salary schedules" and the other two are variations on certain aspects of merit pay.

Special Recruitment Rates for Teachers in Shortage Categories

One of the features of the unified salary schedule that is most often criticized is its requirement that school districts pay all beginning teachers the same salary, regardless of how easy or difficult it is to recruit teachers for particular positions. That requirement, critics claim, is largely responsible for the sometimes-severe shortages of candidates for secondary school mathematics and science positions, whose training allows them to command substantially higher salaries from business and industry. Although the authors know of no direct evidence to substantiate this claim, the comparisons of beginning salaries of college graduates listed in Appendices B and C confirm that graduates with degrees in these specialties do receive substantially higher salaries than their fellow graduates in other degree programs. There is no real reason to doubt that these differentials do generate serious recruitment problems.

The solution often proposed would be to offer candidates in hard-to-fill positions higher salaries, typically by granting them special stipends on top of the regular schedule rates. This seems like such an obvious solution to some observers that the enormity of its implications often escapes notice. Since secondary school teachers with subject-matter concentrations generally have more alternatives on the external labor market than elementary school generalists, the proposal raises the clear possibility that a differential between elementary and secondary teachers would be re-established: a once-common feature that took years to eliminate. In aggregate terms, such a differential would also reopen (or widen) the gap between female and male salaries. And carried to its extreme but logical conclusion, the proposal would represent a return to educational compensation practices that districts began to abandon around the turn of the century: ad hoc adjustment of individual teachers' salaries, with no clear bases for identifying comparable jobs and pay rates in other non-teaching settings and with obvious opportunities for board and administrative abuse.

No other compensation proposal currently being discussed so clearly illustrates the inherent tension between external and internal standards of equity that every employer must face when he or she sets pay rates. Mathematics and science teachers clearly deserve higher salaries than other teachers by any standard of external comparison; they just as clearly do **not** deserve any differential by any standard of internal comparison: their duties, workload, and levels of responsibility are the same as those of other teachers; there is no objective basis for saying that their subjects are more important than any other subject to the education of a district's pupils; and the sums they can command on the external labor market bear no relationship to the quality of their performance in the classroom. For this latter reason, market-based pay is not only inconsistent with the unified salary concept; it is also inconsistent with the concept of merit pay. Merit pay advocates claim that the standardized rates in the unified schedule generate perceptions of inequity among teachers who believe their superior performance deserves greater salary recognition. That problem, if it exists, almost certainly would be aggravated by a system that increased the salience of salary distinctions among teachers without reference to levels of performance.

The previous section outlined a handful of alternatives that might help alleviate the problems of recruiting and retaining teachers in hard-to-fill categories. Guthrie and Zusman (1982) discuss a number of others that do not directly address teacher compensation. But some districts claim they already have made exceptional efforts to fill such positions and still believe that different entry-level salaries are needed. If they are committed to that approach, then they should at least give consideration to structuring it as an exception to the unified schedule, with clear standards established on when such exceptions might be made.

If a district can document that other special recruitment measures have been tried and found insufficient, and if it can establish a credible basis for salary comparisons with other occupations, the district might then be given the discretion to **hire new teachers in shortage categories at a specifed number of steps above step one of a unified schedule.** In effect, new teachers in those categories would be hired with an artificial number of "years of experience." Those already teaching in those categories would receive the same number of artificial experience credits, unless they already had reached the top of the salary schedule.

Such a system would compress the salary schedule for teachers in shortage areas, but it would guarantee that their salaries would be protected if and when the exception is discontinued. Also, if the conditions for making and eliminating such exceptions are clearly spelled out in a negotiated agreement, a union would be able to use grievance and arbitration procedures to police abuses of the system. The Federal civil service system has used a somewhat similar approach for decades, although its approach actually provides for entirely new schedules to be created for shortage positions — a step that would pose greater threats to the basic structure of the unified system.

Pre-Dismissal Withholding of Step Increases

The second alternative to be considered under the heading of limited exceptions to the unified schedule concerns a person who keeps showing up in discussions of merit pay: the incompetent teacher. That such a person does show up, in reference to a program ostensibly designed to reward excellence, suggests that merit pay is probably meant to be more of a stick and less of a carrot than its advocates sometimes care to acknowledge. But the stick in this case is least likely to affect those few teachers who are most likely to need one. Unless virtually everyone in a district were getting merit stipends, there would no reason to believe that the truly incompetent teacher would do anything to try to get a stipend or would be disturbed if he or she did not.

In any case, merit pay opponents argue, school districts already have evaluation and staff development procedures they can use if they want to make some effort to improve the performance of a teacher whose teaching is seriously deficient, and they have tenure hearings and dismissal procedures they can use if a person is beyond redemption. That argument is more to the point than some board members and administrators want to admit. But those who are responsible for administering those procedures also have a point when they assert that dismissal of tenured teachers is an unwieldy device for dealing with questions of incompetence. Administrators can use progressively more severe forms of discipline —oral warnings, formal reprimands, suspensions without pay — to deal with specific rule violations, but lesser forms of discipline are not likely to be of much use when the problem is a teacher's general performance. Dismissal, on the other hand, is so severe that many administrators are understandably reluctant to even initiate it, particularly since they know that charges of incompetence are much more difficult to document than charges of rule violations. What is needed, some educators argue, is something that would serve as the functional equivalent of pre-discharge discipline, to handle cases of teacher incompetence.

To deal with such cases, districts could **give administrators discretion to withhold step increments under the unified salary schedule, under carefully-specified conditions, when a teacher's performance would otherwise warrant dismissal.** These conditions should include: a) a teacher has already been put on notice that his or her performance is seriously deficient; b) has been given a clear understanding of what he or she must do to bring performance up to minimally acceptable standards; c) has been given time but has failed to take sufficient remedial action; and d) has been warned that continued failure to do so will result in dismissal. Withholding a step increment, under such a procedure, would be the functional equivalent of a disciplinary action, entitling the teacher to a hearing before an arbitrator or other third-party neutral. As in other cases of discipline, the burden would be on the employer to prove that such action was justified —that all four preconditions for withholding the increment had been satisfied and that the teacher's performance was so seriously deficient that dismissal would be warranted if it does not improve. In effect, this suggestion would give the teacher the right to a pre-dismissal hearing and one last opportunity to avoid dismissal itself.

The importance of adopting all the elements of this proposal or none at all cannot be emphasized too strongly. Any district that did not put the teacher on notice of specific performance deficiencies, tell him or her specifically how he or she could improve, and give him or her sufficient time and opportunity to do so well before the withholding of a step increment would properly be accused of being arbitrary and capricious. Any district that tried to use step withholding as a less severe penalty for "lesser" degrees of incompetence would undermine the integrity of the unified schedule (not to mention the morale of teachers) and would be telling parents and the general public that the district was prepared to tolerate "some" incompetence among its teachers on a permanent basis. If all elements of this proposal were adopted, the interests of the teacher involved, his or her students, and the district as a whole would be protected. And the district would have more flexibility to deal effectively with genuine incompetence, without making more sweeping compensation "reforms" that cast aspersions on the competence and dedication of the vast majority of its teachers.

Group Bonus Plans

A number of education researchers believe that the traditional approach to merit pay is flawed because it attempts to devise **individual** incentives, geared to **individual** performance (Bruno and Nottingham, 1974). The key to upgrading the quality of education, they argue, is to provide incentives for teachers to act **as a group**, evaluating each other's performance, disseminating new ideas, and working together to solve common problems. They assert that the traditional single salary schedule does not provide incentives for such collaboration, and that merit pay schemes focusing on individual performance positively discourage it.

Specifically, Bruno and Nottingham (1974) propose that school districts adopt **group bonus plans geared to student performance on standardized tests**. The "group" might include teachers and support staff for a particular grade within a school, several grades, an entire school, several schools, or an entire district, depending upon the scope of "collegial team effort" a district wants to emphasize. Bonuses would be distributed evenly (on either a dollar or percentage-of-salary basis) among members of a group, and the size of the bonus would vary depending upon what percentage of a group's students had achieved a pre-determined achievement goal. The school-wide bonus incorporated in the "Houston Plan" follows this general suggestion, although the Houston experiment uses a fixed student achievement target which must be met before any bonus is forthcoming, rather than a sliding scale.

The group-bonus approach would avoid many of the problems that plague traditional individual-based merit plans. It would allow districts to side-step the difficulties of evaluating individual teachers, and administrators would be relieved of the burden of making interpersonal judgments, which too frequently become a source of teacher-administrator friction. Further, it would avoid pitting the interests of individual teachers against one another. In positive terms, the group approach provides incentives for teachers and administrators to work closely together and serves as a vehicle for focusing everyone's attention on achieving school-wide goals and objectives. Such plans are frequently used in certain types of private sector production plants, contexts in which cooperation is important and individual performance is difficult to measure (Lawler, 1971).

Group bonus plans are not without problems, however. They avoid the problems of measuring individual performance, but they force districts to emphasize aspects of group performance that are easily measured. Group plans also encourage teachers to "teach to the tests," and the focus can be diverted from school aspects that need attention but are difficult to measure. While such plans give teachers (and perhaps administrators) additional reasons to focus attention on the achievement of certain school goals and objectives, they also give teachers reasons to **resist** goals and objectives that are particularly challenging. Teachers will realize that their chances of receiving monetary rewards will vary inversely with the difficulty of achieving the pre-set targets. Further, while group plans promote **within-group cooperation**, they also tend to raise **between-group competition**. Thus they can produce problems in coordinating the individual schools in a district. The group plans do not overcome the problem that is ultimately responsible for the friction and non-cooperation that merit pay plans typically generate in public education. That is, the total pool of money for merit payments cannot normally be increased by improved performance — thus the participants are left with the conflicts inherent in a fixed-sum game.

These drawbacks of group-level bonus plans are probably sufficiently serious to outweigh their benefits, but if the group concept is to be pursued, there are at least ways of minimizing its problems. **District-wide bonus plans administered by State-level agencies** would almost certainly be preferable to school-level or grade-level plans administered by individual districts, simply because intra-district coordination is so much more critical than coordination across districts. The advantages that some districts might enjoy because of high local tax revenues and high socio-economic status could be mitigated if bonuses were not linked to fixed achievement test targets, but were linked to **improvement** in test scores over previous performance: those districts with the poorest test scores would have the most to gain by participating in such a program. Using improvement in test scores, rather than fixed targets, would also minimize the incentives for school members to resist setting high standards and difficult goals for themselves.

Alternatives: Career Ladders and Career Promotions

Next to merit pay, the most widely-discussed suggestion for modifying the existing compensation system in teaching has been the suggestion that school districts adopt some form of **career ladder** for their teachers. Career ladder proposals, like merit pay proposals, link salary determination in part to assessments of a teacher's competence or performance, but unlike merit pay proposals they are not premised on the assumption that all teachers know —or should know — exactly how they ought to perform from the moment they first enter teaching. In fact, in this respect, the career ladder concept has more in common with the unified salary schedule than it does with merit pay. Career ladders and the unified schedule both reflect the assumption that teachers cannot be expected to be fully competent when they first begin teaching. Both approaches assume that teachers will acquire competence over time, and both are meant to recognize professional growth with increasing levels of salary.

Unfortunately, the career ladder concept almost always gets confused with the concept of **differentiated staffing**. The basic feature of differentiated staffing is a **job ladder**: a hierarchical ordering of separate jobs, with distinctly different sets of responsibilities. Under the typical differentiated staffing plan, the single job of "teacher" would be broken up into different jobs that then would be ranked according to their level of professional responsibility. The basic tasks of classroom teaching would be grouped in one job and lodged in the middle of the hierarchy. Teacher aides and assistant teachers would occupy lower rungs of the ladder, while those persons at the top would have responsibility for functions such as course development, program evaluation, and teacher training. Although those at the highest levels might continue to spend a portion of their time in the classroom, their basic functions would be coordinative and quasi-supervisory. Such a job ladder, in other words, is a bureaucratic device for organizing and controlling the work done in an organization.

Despite the claims of some advocates of differentiated staffing, a job ladder is not a career ladder. Some people might aspire to promotion up a job ladder — and they might think of it as a career ladder for that reason — but if too many people define career progress in terms of promotion up a job ladder, many of them are going to be sorely disappointed. Many of them will **not** be promoted, not because they are incapable of performing at the higher level, but because there are not vacancies for them at the higher level or because someone else has beaten them out for a promotion. Those who fail to secure promotions, or who **want** to be fulltime classroom teachers, are left in positions that the system defines as less than "fully professional".

The idea of a career ladder is different. Promotions in a career ladder are made when a person is ready for them and are not limited by a fixed number of positions, by turnover in those positions, or by peer competition. In fact, career ladder promotions need not represent promotions to distinctly different positions at all. There is likely to be some differentiation in the tasks that those at different levels perform. In teaching, for example, a beginning teacher could hardly be expected to play much of a role in helping other beginning teachers learn how to teach. The basic distinctions between different levels of a career ladder, however, would not turn on the **tasks** that those at different levels perform, but on what the system **expects** of them when they are performing those tasks. Those at lower levels would not be expected to be fully competent at every aspect of teaching; they would be expected to be **acquiring** competence. As they acquire and demonstrate competence at more and more aspects of their jobs, their discretion would increase, the amount of supervision they receive would diminish, the kinds of training they receive would change, and they would receive promotions and salary increases in recognition of their growing competence and contributions to the organization.

These comments leave several questions unanswered. How many steps should there be to a career ladder in teaching? What criteria would be used to determine different levels of competence? How would judgments of competence by made? **Who** would make them? We will suggest some possible answers to those questions, but our suggestions are only meant to indicate some of the issues that school boards, administrators, teachers and their unions ought to be considering. The issues are not new; in many cases they already may have received explicit attention. The value of the career ladder concept is that it encourages parties to recognize and consider how different issues and different parts of the system affect one another. When the parties address the question of designing and implementing a career ladder in those terms, they often discover that many elements of a career ladder are already in place.

The Tenure Decision as a Career-Ladder Step

Virtually every school system in America already has a two-step career ladder of sorts: the distinction between untenured and tenured teachers. Unfortunately, most people think of the tenure decision almost exclusively in terms of the extra measure of job security that it confers. The fact that it is supposed to mark a transition in a teacher's career from apprentice to journeyman often goes unnoticed. Too often, tenure decisions are *pro forma*, the criteria that are used to make them are vague, and their only practical significance is how they affect job security. If school systems would **formalize criteria for granting tenure** and **give a substantial salary increase when a teacher receives tenure**, both teachers and the general public would be encouraged to think of the tenure decision as a symbol of increased competence and career progress. The salary increase would not replace steps in the unified schedule, but would be a supplement added to the salary of each tenured teacher.

Pre-Tenure Internships

Lack of formal criteria and lack of salary recognition are not the only reasons people do not think of tenure decisions in career-ladder terms. The most important reason is that far too many school districts treat their beginning teachers as if they were journeymen from the moment they are employed. They are assigned classrooms or classes of their own, are given nearly as much discretion as any other teacher, get only slightly more supervision and training, and often are criticized for making mistakes that a system ought to expect them to make. These generalizations are more accurate for some school districts than for others, of course, but most districts would benefit if they were to give explicit attention to how they might **turn the pre-tenure period into a period of genuine apprenticeship or internship**.

First-year teachers could be assigned to work with an experienced, well-respected teacher and not be assigned a classroom of their own until their second year of employment. Teams of experienced teachers might be established and given time to serve as mentors for interns. Special seminars might be instituted to allow interns to share their experiences, discuss common and special problems, and learn how more experienced teachers have dealt with such problems. Where state certification procedures permit, cooperative programs might be established between school districts and schools of education, whereby the first year of employment would also serve as the fifth year of an extended college program. Those who work in a school district probably can think of even more creative ways of turning the pre-tenure period into an internship. What we mean to stress here is the need to think of the period in those terms, and the need to reflect that thinking in the kinds of discretion, training, supervision, support, and compensation we give our beginning teachers.

There is a weakness in the line of argument made above. If teachers are encouraged to think of the tenure decision as one marking an important transition in their careers — and if that is the **only** transition that the system recognizes — then the system, by implication, will be saying that a teacher's career progress comes to an end after four or five years in the profession. When the issue is framed in those terms, some districts might decide they would be better off not encouraging their teachers to think of their career progress at all. The question is debatable, but it prompts another query: are there ways of giving teachers a sense of continued career progress, even after they have been granted tenure? There are two ways of doing so that would involve teacher compensation.

Sabbatic Leave

The first approach, already used by many school districts, would be to **make sabbatic leaves available to all tenured teachers on a periodic rotating basis**. Sabbatic leaves can be used as a form of recognition and as a way of encouraging teachers to pursue research, education, or (sometimes) employment that would enhance their skills and yield special benefits to the district. There are a variety of ways in which sabbatic leave programs can be structured. Teachers could receive full, partial, or no pay for a full or half year. (We doubt that unpaid sabbatics would have any useful recognition value.) Leaves can be available to all teachers as a matter of right, or only to those teachers submitting proposals indicating that leave time would be spent doing something that would yield special benefits to the district. If special proposals are required, the responsibility for approving and rejecting them can be assigned to a committee of teachers and administrators or to a committee composed only of teachers. The program can stipulate that leave time may not be used to accept alternative employment but must be reserved for study and/or travel, or employment of certain types may be permitted (usually with some proportional reduction in the district's salary contribution).

Each of these alternatives has advantages and disadvantages, most of which are fairly obvious. For our purposes, the important point is to recognize that sabbatic leaves can be used as a device for encouraging teachers to upgrade their skills, for giving them recognition and a sense of career advancement, and for strengthening a district's overall educational programs.

Senior Teacher System

The second approach would represent a significant change in the structure of teaching careers, although not as substantial a change as that recommended by advocates of differentiated staffing. The suggestion would be to **add a third step to the teaching career ladder, accompanied by a second significant salary supplement**.

The kinds of criteria districts employ in making tenure decisions will decide, at least in part, whether or not they should take this approach. If tenure is meant to certify that a person is competent in all aspects of teaching, then there would be no justification for creating another step to the career ladder. But if tenure is meant to signify that a person is competent to organize and manage what goes on in his or her individual classroom, then a second set of criteria — marking a transition to a third step of a career ladder — is available: demonstrated ability to make professional contributions to the work of the school or school system as a whole.

Such contributions might include working closely with beginning teachers, developing new curricula, or developing and providing in-service education courses for fellow teachers. They would include anything that strengthens the educational program of the school or district as a whole. These types of contributions might be made outside the classroom, but they could just as easily be made within the classroom. An English teacher, for example, might develop units that reflect and reinforce concepts that are being covered in science or social studies classes; an art teacher might teach special units on architectural history in a history class. The point of emphasizing contributions "to the school system as a whole" is not to suggest that "mere" classroom teaching is less than fully professional, but to emphasize that once a person has developed sufficient skills in the classroom, he or she should be expected to find ways of putting those skills to the widest possible use. Different teachers will have different skills, and different ways of "putting them to use" would therefore be appropriate.

There are three fundamental differences, then, between this proposal and proposals for differentiated staffing, master teacher, and mentor teacher plans that are being considered by several state legislatures. First, under the proposal made here, there would be no quota or limitation on the number of teachers who could be promoted. Second, making contributions beyond one's immediate classroom would not be something a teacher does after being promoted to Senior Teacher; promotion would depend upon a teacher already having demonstrated that he or she can make — and has made — such contributions. Third, promotion would not depend on a teacher demonstrating the ability to perform any particular task that a legislature has prescribed or a principal has assigned; it would depend on a teacher finding ways of turning his or her own strengths into contributions that help integrate and strengthen a school's total program.

Despite the many differences between this career promotion proposal and proposals for such things as merit pay or differentiated staffing, there is still one element that our proposal has in common with others, and it is this element that would give teachers and many administrators their greatest cause for concern: salary advancement would not be completely automatic, but would be based, in part, on assessments of competence and performance. Those assessments, moreover, would not be based on easily-measured, readily-observable factors; they would call for difficult judgments of a teacher's overall competence and contributions, both within and outside the classroom. The absence of quotas would avoid many of the evaluation problems that other proposals generate. (A district that is not prepared to budget sufficient money to give every teacher a career promotion when he or she first becomes eligible should not even **begin** to consider the suggestions we have made in this section). But there still would be a measure of subjectivity to the competence determinations in a career promotion system — a powerful reason to be cautious.

The most sensitive issue remains: *who would decide the promotions?*. If promotion from intern to journeyman were linked to the tenure decision, most states would require that the school board have the final say, and boards probably would insist on retaining the same authority over promotions from journeyman to senior teacher. The real issue, though, is who would make recommendations to the board. The fact that principals and superintendents usually now serve that function in tenure decisions does not mean that teachers would readily accept such an arrangement under a career promotion system: the stakes are raised when salary increases are brought into the picture.

There are three approaches that could be used to make competence determinations in a career promotion system. First, **administrators could make the initial determinations and teachers could be given the right to challenge or grieve their judgments.** An important objection to adopting this approach is its inconsistency with the concept of professional responsibility which the system is meant to promote. Lodging the authority to make competence determinations in an administrative hierarchy would raise all the problems of administrator-teacher antagonism, blocked communication, and so on that cripple merit pay systems. It also would reinforce the top-down control mentality that has encouraged teachers to think of responsibility for anything outside their classrooms as something to be avoided. The only party who might find some comfort in such a system would be the teachers' union, for there would not be much question on whose "side" the union stood if an evaluation issue were framed in teacher-versus-administrator terms.

A second approach would be to **assign responsibility for competence determinations to a committee of teachers or (perhaps) teachers and administrators.** One of the distinguishing features of a profession is that its members take responsibility for evaluating the competence and upgrading the skills of its own members. If a parallel is to be drawn to other unionized occupations, then the same can be said about a craft. Whichever parallel is drawn, it is difficult to escape the conclusion that a true career ladder in teaching would have to involve some form of peer review. Formally involving teachers in the review process would reinforce the principle of professional responsibility. Using a committee, rather than a single individual, would provide a measure of protection against individual bias and subjectivity, and would reduce (but not eliminate) the potential for interpersonal friction that is inherent in any assessment of competence. If the teachers who sat on the committee were elected by their peers (as they are under California's new Mentor Teacher system) the principle of professional responsibility would be strengthened even more. Electing members of the committee also

58

would protect the integrity of the union as a representative of all teachers: the union could bargain over the basic structure of the system and could represent the individual teacher's interests if there were any question of his or her **procedural** rights being infringed, but the union would be neither responsible for nor in a position to challenge the **substantive** judgments of committee members.

A third approach would be to **leave responsibility for tenure recommendations (and promotion from intern to journeyman teacher) with administrators, but use the committee approach for promotions from journeymen to senior teacher.** The rationale for treating the two decisions differently would be that the first decision has direct implications for whether a teacher will continue to be employed, and can reasonably be considered an extension of the hiring process. There is no inherent reason why teachers should not have a voice in the hiring process, but some school boards probably cannot accept such a proposition. They could not raise the same objection in the case of the second promotion, which would not have any implications for job retention.

All three of these alternatives have weaknesses that ought to give school districts reasons to hesitate before committing themselves to a system of career promotions. But a system of career promotions using any of these alternatives would still be preferable to any system of merit pay or differentiated staffing. Note, moreover, that most of the suggestions we have offered in this section can be considered separately, even though there is a common thread that connects them all.

Alternatives: Goal-Oriented Management and Participation Systems

We have discussed to this point specific ways in which school districts might modify their compensation systems to strengthen their educational programs. We now want to discuss a more general approach to achieve the same end: an approach that would be **compatible** with most of these compensation suggestions, but one that would not **require** any modification of the compensation system.

We have made an effort in this monograph to set forth all the basic arguments raised by advocates and critics of merit pay. We have done our best to do justice to all those arguments, despite our obvious skepticism about the feasibility or appropriateness of merit pay. We have acknowledged, where we thought it appropriate to do so, that the problems merit pay is supposed to address are real ones, even if merit pay might not be an effective or appropriate solution to those problems. We have discussed alternatives we think might be more effective and appropriate, despite our own misgivings about some of these alternatives. But we have made no effort to disguise our conviction that the unified salary schedule, as presently constituted, is actually a much more effective and appropriate system than most observers are prepared to acknowledge. There is no evidence that the unified salary schedule causes any of the problems merit pay advocates have pointed to. It is a mistake, therefore, to assume that the solution to those problems must necessarily involve a change in how we administer teacher compensation.

A compensation system is a tool — one of several tools —for managing the relationships between individual employees and the organization that employs them. Whether an organization should try to use its compensation system to resolve problems should depend in part on how using that system would affect all the other managerial tools that the organization has at its disposal. It should depend on some overall strategy for managing the organization. Remarkably, the recent reports concerning education reform rarely mention, except by implication, the question of how our schools are or ought to be managed. They pay too little attention to the interaction between major processes such as compensation and inter-teacher cooperation, and they give too little thought to the managerial strategies in public education.

One reason the commissions and task forces that have issued those reports may have avoided these broader issues is that there is little consensus about how our schools ought to be managed. More often than not, discussions of school management focus on the differences between two models, one bureaucratic, the other professional. The bureaucratic model implies clear lines of authority: delegation of responsibility; rules formulated by superiors to govern subordinate behavior; and centralized evaluation, planning, and decision-making processes. The professional model emphasizes the autonomy of teachers in their individual classrooms. Teachers are seen as being independently responsible for identifying student needs and developing appropriate solutions, functioning within a supportive structure that provides them with the resources they need to fulfill their professional responsibilities.

Few people would argue that either of these models provides a realistic description of how schools actually operate. Our schools are neither tight bureaucracies nor collections of autonomous professionals. They are loosely-knit systems, in which individual teachers have considerable discretion not only over how they organize and perform their work but over what work they decide to perform. They need that discretion, because they are the only ones with direct and on-going contact with the organization's clients, because those clients' needs and abilities are both varied and variable, and because strategies for meeting those needs and capitalizing on those abilities are usually not readily apparent. But that is only half the picture; the other half is that no one individual has complete responsibility for providing services to the organization's clients. Education is not a product one teacher provides to one group of students at one point in time; it is what students acquire over many years, as they move from classroom to classroom, grade to grade, and building to building. As noted earlier, if a school is to avoid confusion and wasted resources, there is a need for coordination and cohesiveness among the individual efforts of teachers and other school professionals.

Bureaucratic and professional models both are used in discussions of school management because each addresses one of two critical needs: the professional model emphasizes the need for teachers to have discretion over how they plan, organize and conduct their work; the bureaucratic model emphasizes the need to coordinate the activities of teachers and other school professionals. Each model, however, emphasizes one need **at the expense** of the other. Bureaucracy serves the need for coordination by limiting and controlling the amount of discretion that lower-level members of the organization exercise. Professional autonomy is defined in terms of freedom from such controls. How these models influence thinking about school management depends upon whether they are considered ideals or reference points for ad hoc decision-making.

As ideals, the two models are bound to generate conflict. Administrators who perceive most clearly the need for coordination and teachers who feel most keenly the need for individual discretion are led to perceive each other as natural adversaries. At best, they can expect to maintain a form of armed truce, under which neither set of needs is completely satisfied; at worst, their separate efforts to serve one or the other need are interpreted as attacks on the other's efforts, provoking counter-attacks that merely undermine **both** parties' effectiveness. Energy and expertise needed for the professional exercise of discretion or the achievement of efficient coordination are diverted to defensive purposes. Trust is undermined.

The armed conflict analogy can be carried too far, however. Most administrators would concede that teachers need a degree of discretion to function in their classrooms, and most teachers would concede that there must be some coordination of their individual efforts. The real problem is not that either group is exclusively wedded to the bureaucratic or professional autonomy model. Rather, it is that both groups believe the only realistic approach to school management is a watered-down combination of both. The ideal models thus become polar reference points for evaluating day-to-day compromises: there may be friction over which concern deserves more emphasis in specific situations, but there is general agreement that there must be some compromise. The more coordination, the less discretion; the more discretion, the less coordination.

Such thinking necessarily excludes the possibility that a school system can attain a high degree of coordination and still give its teachers substantial discretion. **But the school effectiveness literature of the last decade tells us that such educational systems do in fact exist.** That literature also shows that such systems are demonstrably more effective than others in providing their students with high quality educations. If we can identify the factors that have permitted schools to accomplish such results, we will have gone a long way toward formulating a new strategy of school management.

Unfortunately, the school effectiveness literature does not provide cookbook solutions: the research has produced **descriptions** of schools that are particularly effective, but not many definitive **explanations** of how they became effective. Still, the descriptions provide some powerful clues. Principals in effective schools are invariably characterized as "strong leaders", but their strength does not appear to lie in their status or in how effectively they control the activities of individual teachers. In fact, such principals appear to make conscious efforts to minimize status differences between themselves and their teachers, and to avoid dictating solutions to problems or limiting the discretion of their teachers. What they do, instead, is assume primary responsibility for certain key **processes**, insisting that teachers also assume responsibility for participating in those processes and for helping make the decisions that those processes generate.

The processes that appear to receive most attention in effective schools are: (1) goal-setting, in which goals and objectives for the school as a whole are generated and revised; (2) close monitoring and evaluation of programs, curricula, individual student progress, and individual teacher performance, through informal as well as formal procedures; and (3) staff development, not confined to formal training sessions, but pursued through day-to-day exchanges of information between teachers and administrators and among teachers themselves.

These general comments provide the rough outlines of a new model of school management. Administrators in effective schools appear to have given up the notion that coordination necessarily implies and requires top-down controls, and teachers have accepted much of the responsibility for coordination themselves. In doing so, teachers have given up the notion that their need for discretion entitles them to act as independent agents in their individual classrooms. Their responsibility is not to their principals or to their "own" students but to their school and all its students. That responsibility is defined by the goals and objectives that teachers and administrators have mutually agreed will guide their separate and collective efforts. Those goals and objectives provide the basic yardsticks for monitoring and evaluating what goes on in the school and for defining what sorts of staff development need to occur.

The existing research literature does not **prove** that this strategy for managing schools will definitely produce the most effective schools. The strategy outlined extrapolates from a loose body of descriptive material. Still, this explanation of effectiveness in schools is consistent with the great majority of the research findings. It is also consistent with an entirely separate body of theory and research on organizational effectiveness in private sector organizations. Academic research and such popular books as *In Pursuit of Excellence* (Peters and Waterman, 1982) and *Theory Z* (Ouchi, 1981) are generating a model of goal-oriented management and participation systems that is remarkably consistent with the model that (we claim) is being generated by school effectiveness researchers.

These bodies of literature do not provide neat prescriptions or formulas for improving the quality of education. They suggest that teachers and administrators have many of the resources and much of the information needed to find their **own** solutions. If parents and other members of the general public are also involved in the goal-setting process — the linchpin of this new model — then all the critical parties in school districts should be able to work together to achieve excellence in education. The fact that none of this literature makes any mention of schools or other organizations using their compensation systems to promote effectiveness does not mean that there might not be ways of using a teacher compensation system to do so. But that literature makes it clear that **whatever changes are made in the management of our schools should be the product of cooperative agreements and mutual problem-solving**. Changes that one party must impose on others are, almost by definition, changes that will undermine the effectiveness of our schools.

Appendix A

Major Reports on Education, 1983

Source and Title	Main Recommendations
National Commission on Excellence in Education. *A Nation At Risk: The Imperatives for Educational Reform*	Merit pay. "Back to basics". Longer school day and school year. More homework. Better discipline and attendance policies. More reliance on standardized tests. Higher college admission standards. Market sensitive salary schedule (i.e., salaries dependent on demand and supply for particular specialities such as math). Develop career ladders distinguishing between beginning, experienced,and master teachers. Master teacher involvement in teacher training. Raise teachers' salaries to "competitive" levels.
Education Commission of the States, Task Force on Education for Economic Growth. *Action for Excellence*	"Back to basics". Provide students with better computing and problem solving skills. Cooperative activities between businesses and schools, such as team teaching and courses held at worksites. Business-sponsored recognition of "outstanding teachers". Stricter requirements for discipline, attendance, homework and grades. Longer school day and school year. Longer teacher contracts. Close "teacher gap" by higher teacher salaries overall and higher salaries especially for high-demand specialities. Merit pay. Teacher (non-administrative) career ladders.
Carnegie Foundation, author: C. Emily Feistritzer. *The Condition of Teaching: A State by State Analysis*	Teacher salaries and the status and prestige of the profession urgently need to be improved.
Carnegie Foundation, author: Ernest Boyer. *High School: A Report on Secondary Education in America*	More demanding curricula. Mastery of the English language as the central objective. Increase teacher salaries by 25% beyond the rate of inflation by 1986. Improve teacher working conditions (by exempting them from monitoring and paperwork duties for example). Facilitate recruitment of outstanding students into teaching (e.g., offer full tuition scholarships). Improve the education level of teachers by requiring "a sharply focused major in one academic discipline, not in education" (pp. 307-312) Non-administrative career paths. Standardized teacher certification testing in all States. Salary increases tied to career advancement.

National Science Board, Commission on Precollege Education in Mathematics, Science, and Technology. *Educating Americans for the 21st Century*

Establishment of 1000 "exemplary" schools, at both the primary and secondary levels, that would stress education in mathematics, science, and technology. "Excellence in teaching" should be rewarded. High quality teachers should be able to obtain higher salaries without leaving the classroom. In contrast to most other reports, the NSB Commission included expenditure recommendations: $1.5 billion initial cost to be borne by the federal government (around $800 million specifically for the exemplary schools).

John C. Goodlad (former dean, Graduate School of Education at UCLA). *A Place Called School*

Fewer hours of instruction during the school day, giving teachers more time to participate in curriculum development and school management. Differentiated staffing, with hierarchy ranging from teacher aide through "career teacher" and "head teacher" (but opposes merit pay). Head teachers would need to hold doctorate degree and have "special qualifications", rather than gain the position simply by seniority. Head teachers would serve as "heads of teaching teams", provide the teams with "inservice assistance", diagnose "knotty" learning problems, and perform other monitoring functions. Substantial pay differentials between top and bottom levels of the school hierarchy.

Congressional Merit Pay Task Force, chaired by Rep. Paul Simon (D.-Ill.), and including Ernest Boyer (Pres., Carnegie Foundation), Mary Hatwood Futrell (Pres., NEA), Albert Shanker (Pres., AFT), several superintendents and teachers, selected public officials, and representatives from large educational associations. *Congressional Merit Pay Task Force Report*

Thirteen recommendations, including: raise pay for all teachers, especially entry-level salaries; competency test in teacher's major subject area as a condition of employment; scholarships for future teachers; fellowships for especially talented teachers, in order to take study, research, or travel leaves; summer institutes to upgrade the skills of veteran teachers. The Task Force report stated that it supported **experiments** with merit pay (some members wholeheartedly advocated merit pay, others had reservations or were opposed).

Appendix B

Relationships Between Average Beginning Salary Offers of Bachelor's Degree Candidates Entering Business and Industry, by Curriculum, and Average Minimum Salaries of Teachers with a Bachelor's Degree, 1973-74 to 1980-81

Index: Teachers with a Bachelor's Degree = 100.0

Curriculum field	1973-74	1974-75	1975-76	1976-77	1977-78	1978-79	1979-80	1980-81
Teaching	100.0	100.0	100.0	100.0	100.0	100.0	100.0	100.0
Social Sciences	114.6	112.2	112.2	112.6	110.0	115.1	119.5	108.5
Humanities	107.4	105.4	106.1	105.7	107.3	116.4	119.7	112.1
Agricultural Science	122.0	118.8	116.6	120.5	118.9	123.8	132.9	127.6
Marketing distribution	129.5	116.7	115.0	116.9	118.3	123.1	127.6	130.1
Biological Sciences	111.9	112.5	110.9	115.0	127.7	120.4	129.2	130.7
Business-general	124.8	122.9	119.3	120.9	122.4	130.4	135.8	135.6
Accounting	143.8	143.0	139.3	138.4	138.5	142.8	144.1	144.2
Health professions	113.9	117.5	114.0	116.6	116.9	136.7	128.8	149.3
Chemistry	137.4	139.3	140.7	143.8	146.8	157.7	162.7	160.4
Mathematics	135.9	133.4	134.9	140.0	146.0	156.7	164.4	160.6
Computer science	142.2	142.1	142.1	146.5	156.0	165.8	173.7	169.8
Engineering								
Civil	150.3	155.1	151.6	154.6	158.7	165.9	173.2	178.2
Engineering technology	145.2	147.5	148.2	153.5	158.8	169.6	176.7	180.3
Aeronautical	149.4	156.5	157.8	159.9	166.8	178.1	183.7	181.7
Industrial	152.2	157.4	155.9	164.0	171.4	176.4	184.5	185.4
Electrical	153.3	157.6	158.1	162.4	168.4	179.9	188.4	188.0
Mechanical	155.6	163.5	163.8	167.7	173.0	181.8	189.9	192.1
Metallurgical	ND	164.8	165.9	171.5	174.7	185.8	192.4	193.1
Chemical	162.0	174.3	175.2	181.2	186.4	194.4	200.8	206.5
Petroleum	ND	187.7	191.3	197.2	203.7	212.2	221.5	223.2
Other natural and earth sciences	139.1	145.6	143.0	139.3	152.7	161.9	172.0	186.4

Source: NEA Research Memo, *Prices, Budgets, Salaries and Income* - Spring Issue (april 1982)

Note: Data on non-teacher salaries originally derived from College Placement Council Surveys. Classroom teacher salaries from NEA Research sources.

Appendix C

Relationships Between Average Beginning Salary Offers of Inexperienced[1] Master's Degree Candidates Entering Business and Industry, by Curriculum, and Average Minimum Salaries for Teachers with a Master's Degree[2], 1973-74 to 1980-81

Index: Teachers with a Master's Degree = 100.0

Curriculum field	1973-74	1974-75	1975-76	1976-77	1977-78	1978-79	1979-80	1980-81
Teaching	100.0	100.0	100.0	100.0	100.0	100.0	100.0	100.0
Humanities	119.5	122.0	118.0	117.3	111.7	120.6	131.3	126.7
Social sciences	128.2	124.9	123.6	121.0	122.1	132.9	130.1	127.7
Mathematics	145.6	149.1	159.8	150.1	157.0	159.2	169.0	167.9
Business[3] (nontechnical BA)	165.1	163.8	162.0	164.7	166.0	170.7	180.0	168.5
Civil engineering	154.0	155.0	153.7	156.7	162.1	169.1	175.8	181.1
Computer science	156.5	153.2	154.6	161.2	170.7	179.0	186.3	182.0
Nuclear engineering	ND	158.7	158.5	159.1	164.0	174.7	183.6	185.2
Chemistry	146.8	146.5	151.1	154.1	158.0	164.5	169.3	186.3
Business[3] (technical BS)	172.6	173.5	169.6	175.5	179.4	185.3	197.6	187.0
Electrical engineering	160.6	160.9	161.6	164.7	172.5	183.5	191.7	190.3
Mechanical engineering	159.1	166.9	164.3	168.0	174.1	181.9	189.8	191.7
Industrial engineering	156.5	161.7	157.8	165.0	168.4	177.8	186.6	191.8
Metallurgy	158.1	162.7	164.0	164.1	173.2	181.0	189.6	192.5
Geology & related	ND	ND	160.8	162.5	168.1	178.5	187.8	194.3
Chemical engineering	170.1	171.6	172.3	176.3	180.5	188.6	195.2	201.6

Source: NEA Research Memo, *Prices, Budgets, Salaries and Income* - Spring Issue (April 1982)

Notes: Data on non-teacher salaries originally derived from College Placement Council Surveys. Classroom teacher salaries from NEA Research sources.

[1]One year or less of previous full-time, nonmilitary employment

[2]Teachers receiving MA Minimum are not necessarily inexperienced

[3]Includes Business Administration, Industrial Management, and Commerce

Appendix D
Comparison of Teacher Minimum and Maximum Annual Salaries with Annual Salaries of Other Professional, Administrative, Technical and Clerical Positions, March 1979

	First Quartile	Second Quartile (Median)*	Third Quartile
Drafter I	$7,925	$8,820	$10,382
Key Entry Operator I	7,560	8,447	10,044
Accounting Clerk II	8,030	9,072	10,428
Computer Operator I	8,290	8,880	9,927
Typist II	8,342	9,594	11,327
File Clerk III	8,794	10,020	11,627
TEACHERS (BA MINIMUM)		10,138	
Stenographer (general)	8,820	10,380	12,618
Key Entry Operator II	8,916	10,261	12,283
Personnel Clerk II	8,940	10,219	11,820
Secretary I	8,996	10,011	11,400
Drafter II	9,385	10,428	11,703
Engineering Technician I	9,385	10,428	11.732
Computer Operator II	9,496	10,500	12,393
Accounting Clerk III	9,506	10,871	12,826
Secretary II	9,646	10,980	12,660
TEACHERS (MA MINIMUM)		11,322	
Computer Operator III	10,285	11,627	13,452
Personnel Clerk III	10,428	11,784	13,713
TEACHERS (MA+30 MINIMUM)		12,274	
Stenographer (Senior)	10,428	12,313	14,244
Secretary III	10,860	12,480	14,411
Drafter III	10,992	12,514	14,236
Engineering Technician II	11,100	12,409	13,765
TEACHERS (DOCTORATE MINIMUM)		12,946	
Accounting Clerk IV	11,400	13,200	15,694
Secretary IV	11,971	13,765	15,903
Buyer I	12,000	13,260	15,194
Personnel Clerk IV	12,000	13,556	16,378
Auditor I	12,085	13,200	14,411
Accountant I	12,383	13,595	14,860
Computer Operator IV	12,708	14,340	15,685
Chemist I	12,799	14,225	15,600
Engineering Technician III	13,200	14,860	16,680
Secretary IV	13,200	13,765	18,000
Drafter IV	13,244	14,994	16,998
Public Accountant I	13,495	13,994	14,494
Job Analyst II	13,800	14,494	16.607

	First Quartile	Second Quartile (Median)*	Third Quartile
TEACHERS (BA MAXIMUM)		15,147	
Personnel Clerk V	13,932	16,200	17,580
Auditor II	14,494	16,200	18,000
Accountant II	14,495	16,020	18,444
Computer Operator V	14,495	16,424	18,960
Public Accountant II	14,794	15,504	16,505
Buyer II	15,060	16,848	18,900
Attorney I	15,594	18,048	21,240
Chemist II	15,642	17,176	19,161
Engineering Technician IV	15,840	17,446	19,240
Engineer I	16,200	17,000	18,562
TEACHERS (MA MAXIMUM)		17,678	
Drafter V	16,685	18,666	21,204
Accountant III	17,160	19,127	21,368
Public Accountant III	17,400	18,792	20,004
Engineer II	17,520	18,840	20,400
TEACHERS (MA+30 MAXIMUM)		19,222	
Job Analyst III	17,736	19,792	22,200
Auditor III	17,993	20,074	22,620
Engineering Technician V	18,249	20,148	21,864
TEACHERS (DOCTORATE MAXIMUM)		20,232	
Buyer III	18,760	20,674	23,256
Chemist III	18,792	20,968	22,980
Engineer III	19,872	21,691	23,765
Personnel Director I	19,897	22,439	26,052
Public Accountant IV	20,496	22,991	26,989
Attorney II	21,000	23,496	25,549
Accountant IV	21,561	23,700	26,160
Job Analyst IV	21,600	23,760	26,592
Buyer IV	22,440	25,092	28,260
Chief Accountant I	22,991	26,004	27,024
Chemist IV	23,100	25,320	27,489
Engineer IV	23,496	25,800	28,339
Personnel Director II	24,990	27,489	30,488

*Figures for teachers are *average* minimum and maximum salaries for those with only a Bachelors degree, with a Masters degree, or with a Masters degree plus thirty additional credit hours.

Sources: For teacher salaries: National Education Association, *Salary Schedules, 1979-80,* Table 5, col. 11 (1978-79).

For other salaries: U.S. Bureau of Labor Statistics, *National Survey of Professional, Administrative, Technical, and Clerical Pay*, March 1979, Table 1.

BIBLIOGRAPHY

Adams, J. Stacey. "Injustice in Social Exchange." In *Advances in Experimental Psychology.* Vol. 2 Ed. by L. Berkowitz. New York: Academic, 1965, pp. 267-299.

Adams, J. Stacey. "Towards an Understanding of Inequity." *Journal of Abnormal and Social Psychology.* 67 (1963): 422-436.

Ayllon, T. and N.H. Azrin, *The Token Economy*, Englewood Cliffs, N.J.: Prentice-Hall, 1968.

Boyer, Ernest. *High School: A Report on Secondary Education in America.* New York: Harper and Row, 1983.

Bruno, James, E., and Marvin A. Nottingham. "Linking Financial Incentives to Teacher Accountability in School Districts." *Educational Administration Quarterly* 10 (Autumn 1974): 46-62.

Casey, William F. III. "Would Bear Bryant Teach in the Public Schools? The Need for Teacher Incentives." *Phi Delta Kappan* 60 (March 1979): 500-501.

Chapman, David N., and Malcolm A. Lowther. "Teachers' Satisfaction with Teaching." *Journal of Educational Research* 75 (March-April 1982): 241-247.

Condry, John, and James Chambers. "Intrinsic Motivation and the Process of Learning." in *The Hidden Costs of Reward* (Chapt. 4). Ed. by Mark R. Lepper and David Greene. Hillsdale, N.J.: Lawrence Erlbaum Associates, 1978.

Conte, A.E. Mason. *Merit Pay: Problems and Alternatives.* Trenton, N.J.: N.J. State Dept. of Education, Division of Research, Planning and Evaluation. April 1972. 35 pp. (ED. 064 791).

Davis, Hazel. *Why Have Merit Plans for Teachers' Salaries Been Abandoned?* Public School Salaries Series. Research Report 1961-R3. Washington, D.C.: National Education Association, Research Division, March 1961.

Deci, Edward L. "The Hidden Costs of Rewards", *Organizational Dynamics* 4 (Winter 1976): 61-72.

Deci, Edward. *Intrinsic Motivation.* New York: Plenum Publishing Corp., 1975.

Doremus, Richard R. "Whatever Happened to Kalamazoo's Merit Pay Plan?" *Phi Delta Kappan*, Vol. 63, No. 6, February, 1982.

Education Commission of the States. Task Force on Education for Economic Growth. *Action For Excellence: A Comprehensive Plan to Improve our Nation's Schools.* Denver, Colorado: Education Commission of the States, 1983.

Educational Research Service. *Merit Pay for Teachers.* ERS Report. Arlington, Virginia: Educational Research Service, Inc., 1979.

Feistritzer, Emily C. *The Condition of Teaching: A State by State Analysis.* New York: Carnegie Foundation, 1983.

Festinger, L. *A Theory of Cognitive Dissonance.* Evanston, Ill.: Row, Peterson, 1957.

Garbarino, James. "The Impact of Anticipated Reward upon Cross-Age Tutoring." *Journal of Personality and Social Psychology* 32 (1975): 421-428.

Goodlad, John I. *A Place Called School: Prospects for the Future.* St. Louis, Missouri: McGraw-Hill, 1983.

Griffin, Gary A. "Guidelines for Improving Teacher Quality." *American Education* (November 1982): 28-33.

Guthrie, J.W., and Ami Zusman. "Teacher Supply and Demand in Mathematics and Science." *Phi Delta Kappa* 64 (September 1982): 28-33

Homans, G.C. *Social Behavior: Its Elementary Forms.* New York: Harcourt, Brace and World, 1961.

Hulin, C. L. "Effect of Changes in Job Satisfaction Levels on Employee Turnover". *Journal of Applied Psychology* 52 (1968): 122-126.

Jackson, Philip W. *Life in Classrooms.* New York: Holt, Rinehart and Winston, 1968.

Kazdin, A. E. *Behavior Modification in Applied Settings.* Homewood, Ill.: The Dorsey Press. 1975.

Kershaw, Joseph, and Roland McKean. *Teacher Shortages and Salary Schedules.* New York: McGraw-Hill, Inc., 1962.

Knox, Gerald M. "Merit Pay for the Best Teachers?" *Better Homes and Gardens* 48 (Sept. 1970): 4-8.

Lawler, Edward E., III. *Pay and Organizational Effectiveness: A Psychological View.* New York: McGraw-Hill, 1971.

Lawler, Edward E., III. "Reward Systems". In *Improving Life at Work: Behavioral Science Approaches to Organizational Change* (Chapt. 4) Ed. by J. Richard Hackman and J. Lloyd Suttle. Santa Monica, Calif.: Goodyear Publishing Co., 1977.

Leithwood, K.A., and D.J. Montgomery. "The Role of the Elementary School Principal in Program Improvement." *Review of Educational Research* 52 (Fall 1982): 309-339.

Lepper, Mark R., and David Greene. *The Hidden Costs of Reward: New Perspectives on the Psychology of Human Motivation.* Hillsdale, N.J.: Lawrence Erlbaum Associates, 1978.

Little, Judith Warren. "The Effective Principal." *American Education.* (August-September 1982): 38-43.

Little, Judith Warren. "Norms of Collegiality and Experimentation: Workplace Conditions of School Success." *American Educational Research Journal* 19 (Fall 1982): 325-340.

Lortie, Dan C. *Schoolteacher: A Sociological Study.* Chicago: The University of Chicago Press, 1975.

Mahoney, Thomas A. *Compensation and Reward Perspectives.* Homewood, Illinois: Richard D. Irwin, 1979.

Maslow, Abraham H. *Motivation and Personality.* New York: Harper and Row, 1954.

Mason, W.S. *The Beginning Teacher.* Washington, D.C.: U.S. Department of Health, Education and Welfare, Office of Education, Circular No. 644, 1961.

Mc Dowell, Stirling. "Merit Salaries and Other Devices." *Education Canada* 13 (March 1973): 14-19.

McGraw, Kenneth O. "The Detrimental Effects of Reward on Performance: A Literature Review and a Prediction Model." In *The Hidden Costs of Reward* (Chapt. 3) Ed. by Marl R. Lepper and David Greene. Hillsdale, N.J.: Lawrence Erlbaum Associates, 1978.

McKenna, Charles D. "Merit Pay? Yes!" *National Elementary Principal* 52 (February 1973): 69-71.

National Commission on Excellence in Education. *A Nation at Risk*, Washington, D.C. U.S. Government Printing Office, 1983.

National Science Board Commission on Precollege Education in Mathematics. *Educating Americans for the 21st Century*. Washington, D. C.: National Science Foundation, 1983.

O'Leary, K.D., and R. Drabman. "Token Reinforcement Programs in the Classroom: A Review." *Psychological Bulletin* 75 (1971): 379-398.

Ouchi, William G. *Theory Z*. Reading, Mass.: Addison-Wesley, 1981.

Peters, Thomas J. and Robert H. Waterman, Jr. *In Search of Excellence*. New York: Warner Books, 1982.

Phi Delta Kappan. "In the Long Run, You Get What You Pay For." 61, (Nov. 1979): 154.

Porter, L. W., and R. M. Steers. "Organizational, Work, and Personal Factors in Employee Turnover and Absenteeism." *Psychological Bulletin* 80 (1973): 151-176.

Skinner, B. F. *Contingencies of Reinforcement*. New York: Appleton-Century-Crofts, 1969.

U. S. House of Representatives. Committee on Education and Labor. Merit Pay Task Force. Washington, D.C.: U. S. Government Printing Office, 1983.

Vance, Victor S., and Phillip C. Schlechty. "The Distribution of Academic Ability in the Teaching Force: Policy Implications." *Phi Delta Kappan* (September 1982): 22-27.

Vroom, Victor. *Motivation and Work*. New York: John Wiley and Sons, 1964.

Washington Post. May 22, 1983.

Weaver, W. Timothy. "In Search of Quality: The Need for Talent in Teaching." *Phi Delta Kappan* (September 1979): 29-46.

Weissman, Roxanne. "Merit Pay - What Merit?" *Education Digest* 34 (May 1969): 16-19.

Whyte, William F. *Money and Motivation*. New York: Harper and Row, 1955.

Wood, Fred H., Frank O. McQuarrie, Jr., and Steven Thompson. "Practitioners and Professors Agree on Effective Staff Development Practices." *Educational Leadership*. (October 1982): 28-31

Wynne, Edward A. "Looking at Good Schools." *Phi Delta Kappan* (January 1981): 377-381.